The Hunters

The Stages of Human Evolution: Human and Cultural Origins, second edition, *C. Loring Brace*

Tribesmen, *Marshall D. Sahlins*

The Hunters, second edition, *Elman R. Service*

Peasants, *Eric R. Wolf*

FOUNDATIONS OF MODERN ANTHROPOLOGY SERIES

Marshall D. Sahlins, *Editor*

FOUNDATIONS OF MODERN ANTHROPOLOGY SERIES

PRENTICE-HALL, INC., Englewood Cliffs, New Jersey 07632

Elman R. Service, University of California, Santa Barbara

The Hunters

SECOND EDITION

Library of Congress Cataloging in Publication Data

SERVICE, ELMAN ROGERS
   The hunters.

   (Foundations of modern anthropology series)
   Includes bibliographical references and index.
   1. Society, Primitive.   2. Hunting, Primitive.
I. Title.
GN388.S47 1979   301.2   78–13722
ISBN   0-13-448100-3

© 1979 by PRENTICE-HALL, INC., Englewood Cliffs, N.J. 07632

PRENTICE-HALL
FOUNDATIONS OF MODERN ANTHROPOLOGY SERIES

Marshall D. Sahlins, *Editor*

10   9   8   7   6   5   4   3   2   1

PRENTICE-HALL INTERNATIONAL, INC., *London*
PRENTICE-HALL OF AUSTRALIA PTY. LIMITED, *Sydney*
PRENTICE-HALL OF CANADA, LTD., *Toronto*
PRENTICE-HALL OF INDIA PRIVATE LIMITED, *New Delhi*
PRENTICE-HALL OF JAPAN, INC., *Tokyo*
PRENTICE-HALL OF SOUTHEAST ASIA PTE. LTD., *Singapore*
WHITEHALL BOOKS LIMITED, *Wellington, New Zealand*

Foundations

of Modern Anthropology

Series

The Foundations of Modern Anthropology Series is a documentation of the human condition, past and present. It is concerned mainly with exotic peoples, prehistoric times, unwritten languages, and unlikely customs. But this is merely the anthropologist's way of expressing his concern for the here and now, and his way makes a unique contribution to our knowledge of what's going on in the world. We cannot understand ourselves apart from an understanding of *man*, nor our culture apart from an understanding of *culture*. Inevitably we are impelled toward an intellectual encounter with man in all his varieties, no matter how primitive, how ancient, or how seemingly insignificant. Ever since their discovery by an expanding European civilization, primitive peoples have continued to hover over thoughtful men like ancestral ghosts, ever provoking this anthropological curiosity. To "return to the primitive" just for what it is would be foolish; the savage is not nature's nobleman and his existence is no halcyon idyll. For anthropology, the romance of the primitive has been something else: a search for the roots and meaning of ourselves—in the context of all mankind.

The series, then, is designed to display the varieties of man and culture and the evolution of man and culture. All fields of anthropology are relevant to the grand design and all of them—prehistoric archaeology, physical anthropology, linguistics, and ethnology (cultural anthropology)—are represented among the authors of the several books in the series. In the area of physical anthropology are books describing the early condition of humanity and the subhuman primate antecedents. The later development of man on the biological side is set out in the volume on races, while the archaeological accounts of the Old World and the New document development on the historical side. Then there are the studies of contemporary culture, including a book on how to understand it all—i.e., on ethnological theory—and one on language, the peculiar human gift responsible for it all. Main types of culture are laid out in "The Hunters," "Tribesmen," "Formation of the State," and "Peasants." Initiating a dialogue between contemplation of the primitive and the present, the volume on "The Present as Anthropology" keeps faith with the promise of anthropological study stated long ago by E. B. Tylor, who saw in it "the means of understanding our own lives and our place in the world, vaguely and imperfectly it is true, but at any rate more clearly than any former generation."

Preface

This book is not an attempt to describe and analyze primitive band society so completely that the reader will grasp the whole picture, as though he were taking a lesson in a correspondence school course. My aim is to make the reader sense the flavor and comprehend some of the facts of primitive life, but mostly to emphasize as well as understand the theoretical significance anthropologists attach to it and the analytic devices and ethnological concepts that they use.

In some of the introductory courses that I have taught at the University of Michigan, the emphasis of the lectures has been usually on the conceptual side, the readings mostly descriptive. But I always have wished (especially after the exams) that it had been the other way around. There are two main reasons. First, the practical: The elaboration of a theory or even of analytical concepts is much harder to present orally than are data and exemplification, and students are more likely to take incomprehensible notes—or none at all. Second, the emotional one: Nobody likes to be a bore, or be bored. The best classroom sessions (i.e., the least boring to the students, as well as the ones they get straighter in their notes) were always those that exemplified something concrete about primitive life, displayed a *real* atlatl and bow and arrow, played music, showed pictures, told true anecdotes about real persons. On the other hand, the more abstract the subject, the more the students abstracted themselves.

I decided, therefore, that this book would focus on the general, analytical, theoretical, and conceptual aspect, leaving more of the pleasant tasks to the professor—who, after all, is the one standing up in front of a class. This is but a matter of emphasis, of course, not one of watertight compartmentalization. The book necessarily must present data and offer exemplifications of the generalizations. But the teacher could present many more, and above all make them come alive. Nor is this to say that the teacher should not give any theory at all or not emphasize, rebut, or refine those presented in the reading, for that should be part of the fun. To repeat: It is a matter of emphasis and focus.

Inasmuch as the materials presented here are analytical and the data highly generalized, the book would be best supplemented by other materials that are particularized and personalized. Movies like *The Hunters* (Bushmen), *Nanook* (Eskimo), *Churunga* (Australians), and books like *The Harmless People* (Bushman), *The Forest People* (African pygmies), *Book of the Eskimos* would obviously help.

Chapter 1 lists the best-known hunting-gathering peoples. The appendix gives a cultural digest of these peoples and contains annotated bibliographies listing major ethnological sources for each.

Only a small proportion of the works I have consulted in preparing this book are included in the bibliographies. Such a list would be of enormous length because I have had two years of half-time grants and the help of research assistants to explore the documentary accounts of early European encounters with the hunting-gathering societies considered here. The University of Michigan Behavioral Sciences Research Fund provided half-time leisure for the academic year 1961–62 and the National Science Foundation did the same for 1963–64, as well as financing research assistance. The present book should not be construed as a monograph representing the results of that research, but of course my general sophistication about hunting-gathering societies was increased greatly during those years and I hope it shows. I am pleased therefore, to acknowledge with gratitude the above financial support. I am also very grateful to Professors Marshall Sahlins, Eric Wolf, and Aram Yengoyan for critical readings of the manuscript.

Elman R. Service

Preface to the Second Edition

A primary reason for almost any revision of a textbook after ten or more years of its life is, of course, to attempt to bring it up to date; this is where the main work and time has been expended on the present version. A secondary aspect of revision is a more pleasurable one: to correct errors and awkwardnesses in the reasoning and the writing style. I say pleasurable because, as every author knows, it seems that about one minute after the printed version is in the hands of the public (and reviewers) egregious blemishes are noticed that he could not find in the manuscript. This is a continuing source of pain, and revising thus gives a sense of newborn life and reduction of unhappiness. (Someone said that pleasure is simply a reduction of discomfort or pain, and I believe it.)

This new volume adds a dimension that the first one lacked by paying fuller attention to ecological adaptation, particularly in terms of the influence of the very wide differences in relative sedentism/nomadism that is so characteristic of hunting-gathering society. This can cause great demographic variations in the same group from season to season or year to year and, of course, important and consistant variations from the societies of one region compared to another. This adds an important factor in the creation of cultural differences. Furthermore, there are today many more, and more sophisticated, studies of the relationships between variations in habitat and in the culture of hunter-gatherer societies, and it seemed particularly desirable to use and acknowledge them.

This is an appropriate time to acknowledge the help of my research assistant, Ray Hames, whose ethnological field work was precisely that described above. He has been a great help in many other respects, as well.

Elman R. Service

Contents

The Hunters

One *Introduction*

We cannot know all that we have gained in acquiring civilization until we know what we have lost. One gain is probably obvious enough: the lives of primitive peoples have been described as "nasty, brutish, and short," and civilized man, today, is well aware—perhaps too much so—of the amenities as well as the luxuries that are available to him. And certainly in some important respects we *have* gained: improved diet and housing, medical care, police protection, and some relief from boredom as well as from danger. No need to go on; the declining death rate is not subject to disapproval.

But civilized man is often uneasily aware that not all of civilization is an improvement, although there seems to be very little agreement about what is wrong, unpleasant, or perhaps unnecessary about it—except, of course, for such things as war, crime, and mental illness. And even for these ills there is no obvious panacea. Could it be that civilized people do not understand civilization very well? Most anthropologists are likely to go further. Civilized people do not understand civilization *at all*. They do not even know what it is!

1

How can we know what civilization is until we know what is *not* a civilization? Only if we comprehend the extremes can we gain some grasp of the common humanity found in both civilization and non-civilization, as well as the distinctive characteristics of civilization.

The simplest and most obvious step toward enlightenment is to investigate the lowliest societies known, the primitive hunters, whose culture offers the sharpest contrast to our own. This is not to say that the hunters live in a "state of nature," however, for their culture—small-scaled and simple to be sure—is still a culture. The hunters, as we shall see, are not feral. Their culture and society are rudimentary in certain respects, most obviously in technology and in social complexity, but in some other respects their culture is as elaborate as our own. In many important aspects of etiquette, morality, religion, art, family life, rules and sentiments of kinship and friendship, and in "things of the spirit" generally—all aspects of culture that are not directly responsive to increases in the size and complexity of society—it is not appropriate to use such words as "low" or "rudimentary" in describing their culture. In fact, we could even argue that many important aspects of social life will be more refined in small societies than in large, complex societies. Primitive peoples' lives are usually short, but not always nasty, and never brutish.

It has been said that there are some ways in which one person is like all people and others in which he/she is unlike all other people. A similar truism can be applied to the societies of mankind as well. They are all alike in some respects, yet there are some extraordinary differences. There are two distinct kinds of factors that create the similarities in all societies. First, humanity is a single biological species with therefore the same general physical needs, potentialities, and disabilities. Second, all societies anywhere must have the same minimal functional prerequisites if they are to continue as societies, no matter the differences in scale. The similarities found in the cultures of all societies are due to these general biological characteristics and social imperatives. The dissimilarities, in their grossest respects, are due to different degrees of cultural growth and to adaptive responses to varying environmental circumstances. The enormous differences between modern civilization and the culture of hunters is primarily related to the much greater size and complexity of the former; the differences among the hunting-gathering societies themselves largely issue from adaptive variations.

The natural habitats of the hunting-gathering societies considered here are widely divergent. From the polar regions to the tropical rain forests and from sea coasts to interior deserts are the extremes we shall cover. It is fortunate that there are such contrasts because one of the most interesting things about these hunting-gathering societies is their very considerable similarity in many aspects of culture. If they all occupied rather similar habitats, then we might be disposed to assume that a simple adaptation to similar habitat produced the cultural similarity. There are, of course, cultural differences that are clearly related to differences in habitat, and it would be interesting to factor them out. Unfortunately, this is impossible in a book

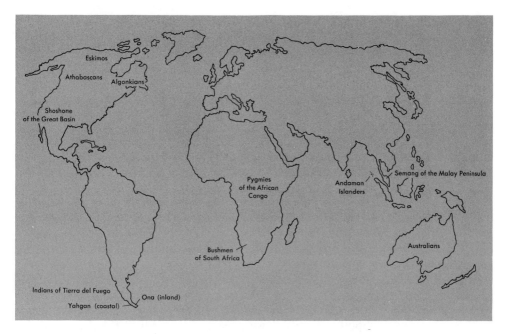

Locations of the major hunting societies of the world.

of this size. We must, therefore, focus on the essential structural or organizational similarity of the primitive bands with only occasional remarks that will point up some peculiarity or striking exception to the generalizations being offered.

Not all the known hunting-gathering societies are included in the present sample. There are sedentary hunting-gathering-fishing societies along the Northwest Coast of North America, for example, which exist in such a bountiful environment, particularly with respect to the resources of the sea, that they far transcend the band level in both demographic and cultural complexity. They should be considered in the context of chiefdoms rather than bands or tribes. Then there are many other hunting-gathering societies which became extinct so soon after contact with civilization that our knowledge of them is too fragmentary. The following are the best-described and therefore the ones anthropologists usually think of when hunting-gathering society is discussed. They are all more fully described in the Appendix: the Eskimos; the Algonkian and Athabascan Hunters of Canada; the Shoshone of the Great Basin; the Indians of Tierra del Fuego; the Pygmies of the African Congo; the Bushmen of South Africa; the Australians; the Semang of the Malay Peninsula; and the Andaman Islanders.

Miscellaneous

The following are hunting-gathering bands, but have not been considered more fully for this work because the information on them is so incomplete.

3

In most cases they were destroyed or drastically acculturated before full studies could be made of them.

Argentinians. The Indians of Argentina, the Puelche, Tehuelche, and Querand resembled the Ona of Tierra del Fuego at the time of the arrival of the Spaniards. They rapidly changed, however, as they acquired the Spanish horse and lived off the proliferating herds of wild cattle in the Pampas.

Californians. In the deserts of southern and Lower California the Indians seem to have resembled the Shoshoneans of the Great Basin in most respects. They were gathered into missions by the Spanish and their culture was thus significantly changed at an early date.

Philippine Negritos. These are Pygmy hunters of the most remote mountains of the Philippine Islands. They apparently resembled the Semang and Andamanese in the eighteenth century, but have since become much reduced in numbers and their culture has changed considerably.

Siriono of Eastern Bolivia. These Indians are interesting because they have been recently studied by a trained ethnologist.[1] They seem to be like some other groups in the Gran Chaco and Matto Grosso, however, reduced from a former more sedentary horticultural form of subsistence to a greater dependence on nomadic hunting and gathering in modern times.

The Band Level
of Society

All the hunting-gathering societies listed above have certain characteristics in common that serve to set them apart from tribal and other higher levels of society. Most obvious and probably most crucial in its effect on the culture generally is the nomadism required by the foraging economy. There is considerable variation, of course, in the frequency and length of their travels, but all band societies move sometimes, and, with the exception of the Eskimos, who utilize boats and dog sleds, the people must themselves carry all their worldly goods. Simplicity and meagerness, therefore, are salient characteristics of the material culture of such peoples.

There is, however, no perfect relationship between economic regime and level of social organization. Sedentary horticultural societies such as some

---

[1] See Allen R. Holmberg, *Nomads of the Long Bow* (Washington, D.C.: Smithsonian Institution, Institute of Social Anthropology, No. 10, 1950).

of the Panoan and Carib-speaking peoples of the Amazon possess a level of social organization at the band level, like the nomadic hunting and gathering bands of Mbuti Pygmies who inhabit the equatorial forests of Africa. Some fully sedentary foraging societies such as the Nootka and Kwakiutl of the Northwest Coast of North America attained the chiefdom level of cultural evolution, a level far more complex than the simple band level exhibited by a large majority of hunting and gathering societies. The exceptional level of development uniformly attained by Northwest Coast cultures was mainly due to a prodigiously rich environment that permitted relatively high population densities (a density probably unsurpassed by any wholly nonagricultural peoples) that inevitably led to more sophisticated levels of integration. Levels of integration beyond the band level were also attained by the foraging Indians of parts of California who depended largely on plentiful acorns for sustenance. Examples such as these are rare ethnographically and need not concern us further. They do not typify the mode of settlement and organization which has characterized human existence for more than 99 percent of its history.

The nomadic way of life mostly influences the social organization. There is, of course, extreme variation in the demographic characteristics of these societies, depending on the kind of food sought, the prevalence of water, and so on. Some of the hunting-gathering societies can accommodate many more people than others, and any of them may vary a great deal from one season to another. But in none of our cases is there any consistent community of a size that rivals even the most modest settlements of horticultural tribes. Obviously, the small size of the community and the low population density means that band society is a simple society, lacking the integrative devices of higher levels of sociopolitical evolution.

The loose integration of families in band society is achieved only by conceptions of kinship extended by marriage alliances. And normally, too, the organization of kin is not complicated by the recognition of the clans and lineages that are so typical of the larger tribal societies. The band is usually a vague entity without very definite boundaries. The domestic family is often the only consistent face-to-face group, although brothers and their families may meet from time to time and sometimes hunt and forage together. The next largest group, the band itself, may take its definition merely from the fact that its members feel closely enough related that they do not intermarry. In some instances they also define themselves territorially, as inhabitants and "owners" of a foraging range. In other cases, joint totemic or ceremonial meetings help set them apart. In any event, marriages which set up or intensify relationships with other bands reciprocally tend to distinguish bands more clearly from one another. The groups, the subdivisions of the society, are thus all familistic, however extended the kinship ties may become.

And finally, band society is simple in that there are no specialized or formalized institutions or groups that can be differentiated as economic, political, religious, and so on. The family itself is the organization that undertakes all roles. The important economic division of labor is by age and sex differentiations; when political functions, such as leadership, are formal they are again merely attributes of age and sex statuses; even the most prominent ceremonies are typically concerned only with an individual's life-crisis rites of birth, puberty, marriage, and death. This fact exemplifies why the band level of society is a *familistic* order in terms of both social and cultural organization.

Two Technology and Economy

People have to eat. Modern people think that they also have a great many other needs. Suburbanites think they need a house, an automobile or two, clothing, electricity, and so on—an enormous list could be made of their needs even were they roughing it in a fishing camp. But obviously none of these are as urgent as food. And the fact of the matter is that food (and water, of course) is the only material necessity that is common to all mankind. Shelter, which would seem to be a universal need, is not required in many areas of the world inhabited by primitive peoples, although usually they resort to some sort of rude hut.

Food, and the few devices employed in obtaining it, is the focus of economic life among primitive bands in a more fundamental sense than it is in more complicated economies. Food-getting is the major enterprise, of course, but more than that, it is a direct confrontation of man with nature. That is to say, there are no specialized groups who get their food indirectly by buying it from the producer or by exchanging services for it in some way. There is no full-time specialization of labor other than the domestic age and

Andaman Islander, whose hunting techniques depended exclusively on the bow and arrow, shooting large fish. (Courtesy American Museum of Natural History.)

sex divisions that are found in any family. Among hunting-gathering peoples this division of labor is simply that men do the hunting, at least the kind of hunting that takes them any distance from the camp. Women, probably because of the relative confinement of bearing and raising children, are left to forage near the camp for vegetable foods and such small game as can be easily caught. But this does not mean that men's hunting is necessarily of greater economic importance than women's work.

"The Hunters" was suggested as the title for this book simply because is sounds more interesting than "Woman's Work," "The Gleaners," or "The Foragers." But in only a few instances (the Eskimos, particularly) is the hunting of animals as productive as the gathering of seeds, roots, fruits, nuts, and berries. Neither men nor women, however, in any society, find their interest much aroused by a description of domestic tasks. "Woman's work is never done," goes the saying, and woman's work is also dull, repetitive, unromantic, and usually unremarked. Is it therefore unimportant?

Dr. R. B. Lee has made one of the most thorough studies of consumption for a hunting and gathering culture, the !Kung Bushmen of Dobe. He noted that meat supplies 37 percent of the diet calorically while the remaining 63

8

percent is vegetable food.[1] However, this figure may be too high to generalize for the !Kung as a whole. J. Tanaka, in an equally detailed study of consumption for the neighboring San !Kung, reports that meat makes up only 18.7 percent of the diet.[2] But both these reports document the fact that food gathering (vegetables) by women dominates the diet of hunter-gatherer cultures other than Eskimos.

Overall there appears to be a strong geographic pattern that determines what fraction of the diet is composed of meat and vegetable foods, and therefore which sex contributes more calories to the total diet. Both R. B. Lee and L. Binford report that as one comes away from the equator (increasing degrees of latitude) the greater proportion of the diet is made up of meat and a decreasing proportion made up of vegetable foods.[3] Since men do nearly all the hunting, they are economically more important in polar regions and correspondingly less important in temperate regions. But meat is an important commodity in any culture and Lee says ". . . the Bushmen of the Dobe area eat as much vegetable food as they need and as much meat as they can." [4] This aphorism probably sums up an attitude towards meat possessed by many hunting and gathering peoples.

A frequent aspect of men's work is its collaborative, or social, character. Woman's work, on the contrary, is often individualized and usually boring. (This seems to be generally true at all levels of cultural development; it is even the common plaint of the modern housewife.) The cooperation of men in the hunt is a normal concomitant of the low state of technological development in band society. A man with a rifle can stalk game by himself and have some chance of killing it, but a man armed with a crude bow and stone-tipped arrows, or with only a spear, needs help. How the team works, of course, depends on the number of men, the kind of game, the nature of the terrain, and their own individual skills and understanding. For example, Tadashi Tanno [5] reports that the Mbuti Pygmy use a kind of net-hunting that involves the cooperation of the entire band, including women (the use of women is quite rare elsewhere). Each man owns his own net which is about 80 m. in length and a number of men cooperate in placing nets to form an open semicircle about 300 m. in diameter. The women's role

[1] R. B. Lee, "What Hunters Do for a Living, or How to Make Out on Scarce Resources." In R. B. Lee and I. DeVore, eds., *Man the Hunter* (Chicago: Aldine, 1968).

[2] J. Tanaka, "Subsistence Ecology of the Central Kalahari !Kung." In R. B. Lee and I. Devore, eds., *Kalahari Hunter Gatherers* (Cambridge: Harvard University Press, 1977) pp. 99–119.

[3] R. B. Lee, *op. cit.*, pp. 30–48; L. Binford and W. J. Chasko, "Nunamiut Demographic History: A Provocative Case." In I. Zubrow, ed., *Demographic Anthropology* (Albuquerque: University of New Mexico Press, 1976), p. 136.

[4] R. B. Lee, *op. cit.*, 1968, p. 41.

[5] T. Tanno, "The Mbuti as Hunters: A Study of Ecological Anthropology of the Mbuti Pygmies." *African Studies* 10 (1976): 101–135.

in the hunt is to serve as drivers. They comb through the forest in the direction of the nets, driving animals before them into the net where they become ensnared, and the waiting men dispatch them with spears and arrows. In a dense tropical rain forest this is the most efficient way to capture game. The Copper Eskimos are notoriously poor archers largely because of the quality of their bows; therefore, whenever the opportunity arises they hunt caribou cooperatively. Asen Balikci reports that this method was much more productive than individualistic hunting.[6] He further reports, in regard to seal hunting, that the method of hunting, either individualistic or cooperative, is dependent on seasonal cycles that relate to the habits of the animals. But in the majority of cases, teamwork is clearly a very significant part of primitive man's hunting method, usually a necessity imposed by the nature of his technology.

The hunting equipment is not so much crude as it is limited. The hunters often travel great distances, and the camp itself is moved so frequently that the material culture—mostly weapons and utensils—must be kept to a minimum. Most of the hunters are familiar with the bow-and-arrow. The Australians are exceptional in this case and use instead a spear with spear-thrower and the unique boomerang,[7] and the Semang jungle hunters use a blowgun and poisoned darts. Traps, deadfalls, and nets are used by several bands, but mostly by the Congo Pygmies who collectively take very large game, even elephants by these means. The Eskimos, given relatively permanent settlements, animal transport, the presence of a great variety of game and fish, plus the Arctic climate, perforce have the most ingenious and complex technology. Hunting equipment ranges from whaling and sealing gear, which features the harpoon with a detachable head, to trident fish spears, the powerful compound bow, and delicately carved ivory fishhooks. Household equipment even includes pottery and stone blubber lamps that also are used for heating and cooking. But all this is exceptional in the world of hunting-gathering bands. Mostly the weapons are so limited that the hunter must make up for his small arsenal by skill, endurance, knowledge, and in many instances by cooperation with others, or at least by freely sharing his game when he is lucky, that he may later receive from others when he is unlucky. This last is an important and major adaptive device that insures a constant flow of meat to members of a camp. Furthermore, it probably is an important reason why people live in groups. It is a way to spread risk and insure survival through cooperation.

Women's food-gathering tasks are not so complicated. Their only tool is a simple sharpened stick used for digging up tubers and some such devices as net bags and bark or wooden bowls for carrying things like seeds, fruit, or nuts. Women and children sometimes collaborate with men during an

---

[6] A. Balikci, *The Netsilik Eskimo*. (New York: The Natural History Press, 1970).

[7] The boomerang, although familiar to modern boys, deserves additional comment. There are two kinds, the heavy non-returning kind that is used as a killing weapon, and the returning kind. This latter is smaller, light, and thin. It is used in games and for diverting flocks of birds into nets that are set between trees.

Congo Pygmy and his wife gathering food. (Black Star.)

"all-hands" type of game drive, armed with clubs in a rabbit drive, or more often stationed at certain places to frighten and thus deflect game toward a prepared ambuscade.

It has been conventionally thought that the productivity of labor in hunting and gathering societies must be very low. For this reason one might suppose that hunting and gathering activities must be nearly unremitting. It has been frequently assumed, in fact, that the hunting-gathering bands are restricted to a low level of cultural development simply because the people lack the leisure to refine or "build" their culture. But self-evident though this judgment may seem, it is nevertheless false. For several reasons having to do with the very simplicity of the technology and the lack of control over the environment, many hunting-gathering peoples work very little. McCarthy and McArthur's time/motion study of Australian aborigines living in Arnhem Land shows that on the average males and females work a little less than four hours per day in order to satisfy subsistence needs.[8] R. B. Lee in a similar study of the !Kung says that males and females work, on the average, only 2.5 man-days per week.[9]

The recent studies of R. B. Lee [10] and J. Woodburn [11] argue that, for the !Kung and Hadza, gathering is significantly more productive than horticulture, in the areas they inhabit. When Lee inquired of the !Kung as to why they did not farm like their neighbors they replied, "Why should we plant when there are so many *mongongo* nuts (the !Kung staple) in the world?" J. Eder, who studied the hunting-gathering Punan of the Philippines, made a careful comparison of the labor returns for gathering and swidden cultivation and was able to quantitatively show that gathering was more productive.[12] The productivity of gathering has led some anthropologists to speculate that hunter-gatherers are the most leisured peoples in the world. However, other studies show that some swidden cultivators spend much less time making a living than do hunter-gatherers. Since there is a tendency for humans to select the most efficient (or easiest) and secure way of providing food for themselves, we believe it is safer to conclude that the food procurement method employed by a people is the most productive for the environment in which they live. This is quite plausible because many hunter-gatherers, where they come into contact with horticulturists, know how to garden. Yet, they retain their traditional mode of life because it is demonstrably more productive. Thus the transition to agriculture from hunting-gathering did not occur because of the invention or discovery of agriculture. The transition undoubtedly was caused by an increase in population that diminished the amount of easily available wild-food resources per person, requiring a much higher input of work to gather the same amount of food. In these circumstances horticulture would prove more adaptive because it was more productive and could sustain a growing population.

The salient technological limitations are those concerned with the preservation and storage of food. Without the refrigerating, canning, salting, or smoking of meat and fish, of course, there is no point in hunting or fishing once a supply is at hand, for it must be eaten soon, even in the driest climates. (The Eskimos, of course, can freeze their food in winter—a most important factor, for it seems clear that if they did not they could not survive a winter in the Arctic.) Most vegetable foods do not store well, either, with the exception of seeds and nuts. Grass seeds, in fact, are tremendously important in many regions simply because they are the "iron ration" that can be kept for the inevitable periods of drought or slack hunting. But most foods will

---

[8] Quoted in M. Sahlins. In R. B. Lee and I. Devore, eds., *Man the Hunter*, "Note on the Original Affluent Society." (Chicago: Aldine, 1968).

[9] R. B. Lee, *op. cit.* Unfortunately, Lee nowhere defines how many hours go into a man-day of labor or whether children were included; this is a serious omission. J. Tanaka (*op. cit.*), who worked with a different !Kung group, reports that adult members of his group worked, on the average, five hours per day.

[10] R. B. Lee, *op. cit.*, 1968.

[11] "Hadza Ecology." In R. B. Lee and I. Devore (eds.) *op. cit.*, 1968.

[12] "Disruption in a Tropical Forest Human Ecosystem: the caloric returns to food collecting." Human Ecology 6(1) (1978): 55–69.

spoil, which means that once a quantity is acquired activity stops until it is all gone, or nearly so, simply because there is nothing to be done with a large surplus.

The lack of control over the environment has a similar effect. Game is either available or not available at any given time—the fish are running, plants are in seed, fruits and nuts are ripe, and roots are edible only during certain seasons and in certain places. When the vegetable foods are available, they are usually *very* plentiful and easily obtainable, or else they are not available at all. Such extremes mean that a group goes after what exists and it is not usually difficult or time-consuming to acquire it; they do no seek nonexistent things. There are, of course, times when it is hard to get enough food and the labor expended may be great, but more usually the situation is polar—some items easy to get, others completely absent.

Lack of control over the environment should not be taken to mean that hunter-gatherers are more poorly adapted to their environment than are horticulturists. The control horticulturists have over the environment is that they are able by planting to produce more food than naturally occurs. However, they do so at an important cost. Most primitive horticulturists depend on one starchy crop for most of their food. Dependence on one crop reduces their intake of crucial vitamins and minerals, which cannot be expected to be supplied by one crop, no matter how calorically rich it is. The naturally occurring foods depended on by hunter-gatherers are usually climax species perfectly adapted to the environment. They are usually better able than crops to withstand environmental stress, and many crops cannot exist without the intervention of man. Finally, the adaptiveness of a hunting and gathering way of life is attested by the fact that humanity has passed more than 99 percent of its history in this state.

Again excepting the Eskimos, the material conditions of life in general are bare of comfort. The Canadian Indians wear caribou-skin tailored clothing, but the other hunting bands go naked. Even in the chill winds of Tierra del Fuego, the Ona and Yahgan Indians protect themselves only with grease. As for shelter, a brush windbreak is built for temporary residence, a low dome-shaped brush hut for a longer stay. Kitchen gear is nonexistent except, of course, for stone cutting tools and in some cases, baskets. Food is simply baked or roasted directly on the coals and ashes of the fire. The only more complicated form of cooking is the stone-lined covered pit used for baking large animals.

Nomadic Patterns

Hunters and gatherers are totally dependent on naturally occurring resources to satisfy all subsistence needs. Therefore, the distribution, seasonality, and density of these resources strongly influence the movement, size, and composition of the band. Their distinctive nomadic way of life is tied to this fact. Examples of this nomadic pattern will be demonstrated by examples of hunters and gatherers living in different biogeographic regions.

The Copper Eskimo live in the Arctic where plant foods fit for human consumption are rare and only available for a few months in the short Arctic summer. By necessity they must depend on animals for over 90 percent of their diet, but the caribou, ringed seal, and fish on which they depend are not present or available in any one place throughout the year. From May through November the Eskimo are divided into small hunting groups of five to twenty members living along the coast and slightly inland in order to fish for tom cod, trout, and char, which are unavailable during the winter months. Toward the end of July, caribou migrate from the south to feed on lichen and dwarf willow. Caribou are hunted extensively at this time because they are plentiful, fat, and their skins are in fine condition for the manufacture of clothing and shelters. In November the weather grows cold and caribou migrate south, forcing the Copper to trap trout and char in fishing weirs as they return to the sea for the winter. During this time (which the Eskimo call the sewing season) they aggregate into larger groups of thirty to sixty people. Although some hunting and fishing is still done, they largely live off cached supplies of caribou meat that tide them through the month while the women make and repair clothing for the coming winter. In December several such minimal bands join together on the sea ice in groups of 100 or more to cooperatively hunt the ringed seal. During this winter period, seals are nearly the only food the Eskimo eat, and securing an adequate supply demands the cooperation of a large number of people. Thus the Copper Eskimo pattern of nomadism is one of oscillation between inland-coastal and offshore sea-ice zones, with corresponding changes in the sizes of the groups.[13]

The nomadic pattern of the G/wi Bushmen of the Central Kalahari described by G. Silberbauer [14] differs radically from the oscillatory pattern of the Eskimo. The G/wi inhabit the great Kalahari desert of southern Africa, and, naturally, the availability of water is a factor that strongly influences a band's movements. They must always locate within walking distance of water.[15] From December to July, when food is most abundant, they travel in groups of fifty to sixty people. Since from 63 percent to 84 percent of their diet is vegetable matter, campsites are chosen for the quality and quantity of plants in the vicinity. Bands remain in these areas for three to four weeks. The duration of the stay is determined by the amount of time women must spend traveling to collect food: In the beginning, food is plentiful near the camp; but as time passes, women must travel farther to gain an equal amount of food, until it becomes more practical to move to an area of unexploited food resources. Whenever there is a superabundance of food, two groups will join together to enjoy a period of welcome and intense social interaction. From late winter to early spring (August to November) seasonal drought and

---

13 The above was abstracted from D. Damas, "The Copper Eskimo." In M. G. Bicchiere, ed., *Hunters and Gatherers Today* (New York: Holt, Rinehart and Winston, 1972) pp. 3–50.

14 G. Silberbauer, "The G/wi Bushmen." In M. G. Bicchiere, ed., *Hunters and Gatherers Today* (New York: Holt, Rinehart and Winston, 1972) pp. 271–326.

15 However, J. Tanaka, *op. cit.*, who studied a different Bushman group, the //Gana San, reports that they do not consume water for 300 days out of every year, instead relying on a melon for 90 percent of their water.

frost reduce the variety and quantity of plant foods so much that the G/wi find it necessary to break up the band into units of twenty people, and later in the season into nuclear family or small extended families of not more than five people widely dispersed over the entire band territory. During this period, Silberbauer remarks, "Plant foods are scarce, the diet is monotonous; hunger and thirst are the common lot." [16]

Two recent studies of the Mbuti pygmies of the Ituri Forest, by R. Harako and T. Tanno,[17] enable us to minutely describe their nomadic round. The great rain forest of Zaire differs greatly as a human habitat for hunter-gatherers compared to the desert and arctic region we have already described. Throughout the year the Mbuti live in one of two types of camps: from August to November, during the heaviest part of the rainy season, the Mbuti live in village camps of forty to sixty people; from December to July, in mobile hunting camps of the same size or larger.[18] The Mbuti have a unique symbiotic relation with Bantu horticulturists of the area. During the heavy rainy season Mbuti depend on crops given to them by the Bantu in exchange for meat that the Mbuti are much more adept at capturing. They live close by the Bantu and do very little hunting because the forest is flooded and difficult to hunt. In December, when the rains abate, they move out into the deep forest, away from the permanent Bantu villages, and resume their normal life. Each band has five or six hunting camps spaced 5–8 km. apart on a line, usually following the course of a small river. Nearly every day most of the adults, except for the elderly who stay in camp and care for children, hunt for about 7½ hours in six or seven different locations. After about a month, game becames scarce and the camp moves to another site where game is more plentiful. When heavy rains return in August, they return to their village camps, completing the yearly circuit.

We have seen that hunter-gatherer movement and population dispersion-aggregation is a result of ecological factors: the rate of movement or duration of sedentism is dependent on the ease of hunting and/or gathering. As Lee [19] has shown, movement does not occur after every edible resource has been exploited, but rather when the effort expended becomes too great relative to the amount of food gained; that is, they try to minimize their subsistence efforts. In terms of an input-output analysis, it is more economical to move to an area that has abundant food because it has not yet been exploited. The phenomenon of fusion-fission (or aggregation-dispersion) is also dependent on subsistence factors: when food is concentrated, band units tend

---

16 Silberbauer, |*op. cit.*, p. 278.

17 R. Harako, "The Mbuti as Hunters: A Study of Ecological Anthropology of The Mbuti Pygmies." *African Studies*, Kyoto University, 10 (1976): 37–99; T. Tanno, "The Mbuti Net-Hunters in the Ituri Forest, eastern Zaire: their hunting activities and band composition." *African Studies*, Kyoto University, 10 (1976): 101–135.

18 Mbuti are of two types: net-hunters and archers. Archers do not hunt with nets; as a result, their settlement pattern is slightly different. Their village camps are slightly larger and hunting camps slightly smaller than those of net-hunters. We shall focus on net-hunters because more study has been done on them and they are more common. Information on archers can be found in T. Tanno and R. Harako *op. cit.*, 1976.

19 R. B. Lee, *op. cit.*, 1969.

to aggregate; when it is scarce and dispersed over a wide area, bands break up into component parts. Again, this is dictated by simple economic considerations that have proved adaptive through time.

Economic Relations

One team of hunters is successful at a time when another probably is not. One camp is in a territory where some seeds, or roots, or whatever, are abundant whereas others are not. Nature provides only sporadically in both time and place. It would seem, then, that because one family or band ordinarily will have an abundance of one kind of thing at one time only, and a scarcity of other things, exchanges of food among groups would not only be advantageous but absolutely necessary.

And the truth is as might be expected. Exchanges are made, and they are necessary, and the people know it. But the forms of the exchange are unusual—to a modern observer, at least. We are accustomed, because of the nature of our own economy, to think that human beings have a "natural propensity to truck and barter," and that economic relations among individuals or groups are characterized by "economizing," by "maximizing" the results of effort, by "selling dear and buying cheap." Primitive peoples do none of these things, however; in fact, most of the time it would seem that they do the opposite. They "give things away," they admire generosity, they expect hospitality, they punish thrift as selfishness.

And, strangest of all, the more dire the circumstances, the more scarce (or valuable) the good, the less "economically" will they behave and the more generous do they seem to be. We are considering, of course, the form of exchange among persons *within* a society and these persons are, in band society, all kinsmen of some sort. There are many more kinsmen in a band than there are people in our own society who actually maintain close social relations; but an analogy can be drawn with the economy of a modern family, for it, too, contrasts directly with the principles ascribed to the formal economy. We "give" food, do we not, to our children? We "help" our brothers and "provide for" aged parents. Others do, or have done, or will do, the same for us. E. B. Tylor once remarked on the relationship of *kindred* and *kindness*, "two words whose common derivation expresses in the happiest way one of the main principles of social life."

Exchanges of goods, favors, and labor take a general form that has been called *reciprocity*, which in turn can be broken down into three varieties: generalized, balanced, and negative reciprocity.[20] Let us pause to define these concepts before proceeding to exemplify them.

Generalized reciprocity is a form of exchange based on the assumption

---

[20] These analytic categories as well as the sense of the following discussion are borrowed from Marshall D. Sahlins, "On the Sociology of Primitive Exchange." In *The Relevance of Models for Social Anthropology*, M. Banton, ed. (Monographs of the Association of Social Anthropologists, No. 1. London and New York: Tavistock, Praeger, 1965), 39–236.

that returns will balance out in the long run. So firm is this expectation that when something is given to or done for another, the matter of return is not specified—ordinarily not even implied. This is, obviously, the way exchanges are made among people who are close kinsmen (or very close friends), even in our own society. It is the form of highest altruism. It is based on the fact that the people who exchange are going to be associated for a very long time. The reciprocity, therefore, is only a very general expectation. "In the long run" things even out. The reciprocity is not explicit; it might be impolite, even insulting, to indicate that a return is expected. Furthermore, the mutual exchange is almost never of equivalents. If your older brother helps put you through college, it may be years before you can help him do something—and what will it be? Probably you will not help *him* through college.

Balanced reciprocity, on the other hand, implies a straightforward and explicit exchange that is (ideally) satisfactory to both parties in terms of the goods or acts themselves. Thus it gives the appearance of being more truly reciprocal, more utilitarian, less personal, and less altruistic than the generalized form. Each party knows what is to be returned for what, and when.

Negative reciprocity literally, of course, would imply no reciprocity at all, or the opposite of reciprocity—theft or the forceful seizure of goods. But because all forms of exchange actually fall somewhere along the continuum from generalized to negative reciprocity, rather than in three closed compartments, there are many cases when there is in fact an exchange but when the intent of either or both parties is to get the better of the other, to acquire an unearned increment with the only cost being the social and emotional one—creating a possible enemy or at least precluding friendship. This, too, is negative reciprocity and the most common form of it in the modern world.

The spectrum of exchanges as defined above is matched by parallels in sociability, etiquette, moral attitudes, emotions, and most obviously, in the actual internal social structure of the community and the relations among communities. Inasmuch as small primitive societies are socially structured entirely in terms of kinship, the simplest way to discuss the social and ideological concomitants of kinds of exchanges is in terms of the kinship order.

The most obvious is that the closest kinship relationship is the one that also admits the most generalized form of reciprocity. The more distant the relationship, the more the tendency to balance the reciprocity. Finally, only strangers or enemies exchange, if they do, unsociably—that is, by haggling, guile, or theft.

At the generalized pole, because close social relations prevail, the emotions of love, the etiquette of family life, the morality of generosity all together condition the way goods are handled, and in such a way that the economic attitude toward the goods is diminished. Anthropologists have sometimes attempted to characterize the actual transaction with words like "pure gift" or "free gift" in order to point up the fact that this is not trade, not barter, and that the sentiment involved in the transaction is not one of a balanced exchange. But these words are not quite evocative of the actual nature of the act; they are even somewhat misleading.

Once Peter Freuchen was handed some meat by an Eskimo hunter, and responded by gratefully thanking him. The hunter was cast down, and Freuchen was quickly corrected by an old man:

> You must not thank for your meat: it is your right to get parts. In this country, nobody wishes to be dependent on others. Therefore, there is nobody who gives or gets gifts, for thereby you become dependent. With gifts you make slaves just as with whips you make dogs.[21]

The word "gift" has overtones of charity, not of reciprocity. In no hunting-gathering society is gratitude expressed, and, as a matter of fact, it would be wrong even to praise a man as "generous" when he shares his game with his campmates. On another occasion he could be said to be generous, but not in response to a particular incident of sharing, for then the statement would have the same implication as an expression of gratitude: that the sharing was unexpected, that the giver was not generous simply as a matter of course. It would be right to praise a man for his hunting prowess on such an occasion, but not for his generosity.

"Gift" or "giving" suggests spontaneity, impulse, even favoritism or, perhaps, the personal dominance of the giver. But in a close-knit community of kinsmen such attributes of the act are inappropriate. *Obligation* and *due* are more apt, because these words better express the fact that sharing is an expectation of the moral order and a rule of etiquette, as well as the keynote of the value system. A man shares simply because it is the right thing to do; he may later receive and this also is his right. It would not do to express this expectation explicitly, however, for it should be taken for granted. As Spencer and Gillen say of the native Australian:

> It is with him a fixed habit to give away part of what he has, and he neither expects the man to whom he gives a thing to express his gratitude, nor, when a native gives him anything, does he think it necessary to do so himself, for the simple reason that giving and receiving are matters of course in his everyday life.[22]

Sometimes you may read that food and perhaps other things are common property in very primitive communities. But this statement too is misleading if it suggests that the community shares equally on any given occasion. The obligations are often specific with respect to particular relatives. Among the !Kung Bushmen of South Africa, for example, parts of a large animal are

---

21 Peter Freuchen, *Book of the Eskimos* (Cleveland and New York: World Publishing Co., 1961), p. 154.
22 Sir Baldwin Spencer and F. J. Gillen, *The Arunta*, Vol. 1 (London: The Macmillan Co., 1927), p. 37.

distributed through a camp in several waves. Initially it is divided among the hunting party, but then these men distribute their portions as follows:

> A man's first obligation at this point, we were told, is to give to his wife's parents. He must give to them the best he has in as generous portions as he can, while still fulfilling other primary obligations, which are to his own parents, his spouse, and offspring [all these people cook meat separately]. He keeps a portion for himself at this time and from it would give to his siblings, to his wife's siblings, if they are present, and to other kin, affines and friends who are there. Everyone who received meat gives again, in another wave of sharing, to his or her parents, parents-in-law, spouses, offspring, siblings, and others. The meat may be cooked and the quantities small. Visitors, even though they are not close kin or affines, are given meat by the people whom they are visiting.[23]

Because food, as opposed to weapons and other durables, is the one great need and because eating together connotes intimate sociability, it is the good that is by far the most frequently shared in order to promote or increase sociability among more distantly related peoples. Durables, on the other hand, are more likely to be exchanged in terms of balanced reciprocity except among very close kin.

Often, of course, exchanges of certain things among non-related bands are extremely important to the well-being of all. But primitive society is not commercial and exchanges of a particular form tend to accompany social relationships of an appropriate intensity. When a consistent exchange is desired by two unrelated parties, and when war is undesirable, then there are several ways to establish the social path along which the goods can move. One extreme is the famous "silent trade," whereby one group leaves something desired by the others in a certain place. Later they return to find what has been left in return. The social dangers inherent in haggle and chicanery are abolished simply by not having any social contacts at all. More usual, however, is to have a marriage, or a trade-partnership, trade-friendship, or fictional (ritualized) kinship bond established between particular individuals of the two societies. They may actually exchange, in a friendly but ultimately balanced way, considerable quantities of goods on behalf of a number of other people in their own groups.

So far, we have spoken mostly of exchange with emphasis on the form of the exchange itself, with social relations treated as an implicit aspect of the process. But the implementation of social relations for their own sake often can be both the function and the purpose of an exchange of goods. And on the other hand, accumulating goods promotes envy and distrust, and at the least reduces the prestige and esteem a person may enjoy. For example, Mrs. Thomas says of the !Kung Bushmen:

> A Bushman will go to any lengths to avoid making other Bushmen jealous of him, and for this reason the few possessions that Bushmen

---

[23] Lorna Marshall, "Sharing, Talking, and Giving: Relief of Social Tensions Among !Kung Bushmen." *Africa*, No. 31 (1961), 238.

have are constantly circling among the members of their groups. No one cares to keep a particularly good knife too long, even though he may want it desperately, because he will become the object of envy. . . . Their culture insists that they share with each other, and it has never happened that a Bushman failed to share objects, food, or water with the other members of his band, for without very rigid co-operation Bushmen could not survive the famines and droughts that the Kalahari [Desert] offers them.[24]

The above passage indicates how generosity is required in order to maintain a status—that is, to prevent jealousy. Another aspect of it, however, is that one can *create* sociability by sharing and thus increase his status. Fellowship can be initiated and fostered as well as maintained by sharing. If the goods shared are needed, if their utility or "value" is high, so much the better, but it is noteworthy that the deed itself connotes the appropriate sentiment even when the thing received is not particularly useful. One may, as a matter of hospitality, offer food to a visitor who had already sated himself elsewhere. The sentiment of friendship is demonstrated nevertheless, so truly, indeed, that it would be a grave breach of good behavior for the visitor not to eat with relish. In the same vein, objects of no utilitarian value whatsoever circulate among groups and are always received graciously. Giving and receiving such things ceremonialize and symbolize friendly relations.

Good manners, in any society, are closely connected with reciprocity, especially when food is involved. So far, you may get the impression that a simple open-handedness is all that our "savages" require of one another. But this is not exactly so and some complications should now be discussed. Radcliffe-Brown has the following to say with respect to the complexity of gift-giving among the Andamanese:

When two friends meet who have not seen each other for some time, one of the first things they do is to exchange presents with one another. Even in the ordinary everyday life of the village there is a constant giving and receiving of presents. A younger man or woman may give some article to an older one without expecting or receiving any return, but between equals a person who gives a present always expects that he will receive something of equal value in exchange. At meetings that take place between neighboring local groups the exchange of presents is of great importance. Each of the visitors brings with him a number of articles that he distributes amongst the members of the group that he visits. When the visitors depart they are loaded with presents received from their hosts. It requires a good deal of tact on the part of everyone concerned to avoid the unpleasantness that may arise if a man thinks that he has not received things as valuable as he has given, or if he fancies that he has not received quite the same amount of attention as had been accorded to others. It is considered a breach of good manners ever to refuse the request of another. Thus if a man be asked by another to give him anything that he may possess, he will immediately do so. If the two

[24] Elizabeth Marshall Thomas, *The Harmless People* (New York: Alfred A. Knopf, 1959), p. 22.

men are equals the return of about the same value will have to be made. As between an older married man and a bachelor or a young married man, however, the younger would not make any request of such a nature, and if the older man asked the younger for anything the latter would give it without always expecting a return.[25]

It is also possible for competition to arise in the context of giving. One might think, but erroneously, that since capitalism is so often equated with "rugged individualism" and competition, the opposite form of exchanges, the generalized reciprocity of primitive societies, must therefore be by its nature always idyllic, loving, and in all respects non-competitive. But relations among competing businessmen are not necessarily angry or bitter, because business exchanges, even when conducted face-to-face, are ideally, at least, and probably mostly in fact, impersonal. But generalized, or even balanced, reciprocity in primitive society is intensely social. Troubles can arise as well in the social aspect of giving as in the purely economic. Even when the aim of the act is to enhance sociability, it is possible to perform it wrong.

We know this well enough in our own society. We know that gift-giving in our own personal social realms can involve sentiments of anger as well as love, envy and competition as well as equality and peace. (If this is not so of your own social life, read *Advice to the Lovelorn* in any daily paper, or consult a book of etiquette. Perhaps it is sufficient merely to mention social-climbers, or the annoyances caused by the ostentation of the gifts given by a *nouveau riche*, or the rivalries of wives as they plan their guest lists for cocktail parties and dinners.)

The very fact that in modern urban life husbands who spend all day in the hurly-burly of the competitive business world are sometimes said to be "nicer" than their gossipy, malicious, envious wives makes a point. If some men are often nicer in these respects than their wives (if, that is, the comparison has some validity beyond being merely folklore invented by men themselves), then it is certainly relevant to remember that women are involved in and given responsibility for the more purely personal-social part of the household's relations with the outside world—and *those* are the touchy relations.

One might expect, therefore, inasmuch as no exchange in primitive society is ever purely utilitarian, but is simultaneously social, that the social nuances and complexities might be greater than in modern urban life. Anyone who has visited a primitive society can tell you that this is so. And it is also true that social competitiveness in the context of the economics of etiquette can sometimes be very strong. As a matter of fact, some primitive societies, like Indian groups of central California, so assiduously practice prestige-grabbing and social-climbing within the economics of gift-giving that they have been described as having a "protestant ethic," "capitalist ethos," and so on, apparently because the competition for status is so great. Competitiveness,

---

[25] A. R. Radcliffe-Brown, *The Andaman Islanders* (Glencoe, Ill.: The Free Press, 1948), p. 42.

individualism, and egotism, however, can characterize endeavors that are not entrepreneurial—individual competition in sports is not confused with capitalism, for example, The competition that exists between individuals vying for status and leadership is *social* in primitive society and the goods used are social capital, not economic capital. The social gains that result in more friends and followers are the consequence of sharing wealth, not putting it in the bank.

At any rate, it is possible to give too much as well as too little, and above all it is possible to give incorrectly. People are very sensitive in this context in any society, and it would seem that this must be the reason why in band society—whose system of generalized reciprocity is so large a part of life—the exchanges are so likely to follow customary norms, as obligations and dues, rather than to resemble the truly spontaneous gift.

Property
in Band Society

The economic relationships in band society seem to contrast utterly with entrepreneurial, or free-market, relationships. The main similarities to modern Western society are found only in the family itself, because kinship relations and the sharing of goods among kin are roughly similar in any society. Because of the evident contrasts with capitalism, the social economy of primitive peoples has sometimes been called communism or primitive communism.

To discuss this question only in terms of the way goods are exchanged would be inadequate, for the matter of property is crucial. "Communism" has several meanings, but they are all based on the idea of public, communal, or state ownership of at least the most important resources and means of production. It is also relevant to discuss primitive property in this context of communism, because primitive societies have so often been cited to prove or disprove "human nature" types of arguments. Particularly, a great many defenders of the rights of property have propounded that there is an "acquisitive instinct," or a "natural love of possession," thus an inevitability and universality about private property because it is simply human nature to desire it.

But first let us clear the air a little. T. E. Cliffe Leslie makes the following very important point:

> Property has not its root in the love of possession. All human beings like and desire certain things, and if nature has armed them with any weapons are prone to use them in order to get and keep what they want. What requires explanation is not the want or desire of certain things on the part of individuals, but the fact that other individuals, with similar wants and desires, should leave them in undisturbed possession, or allot them a share, of such things. It is the conduct of a community, not the inclination of individuals, that needs explanation.[26]

[26] T. E. Cliffe Leslie, "Introduction" to Emile de Lavelaye, *Primitive Property* (London: The Macmillan Co., 1878), p. xi.

The pooling and sharing of goods that we have pointed out in the fore-going discussion is suggestive of the nature of property in primitive society. Individuals obviously must *have* the goods before they can share them, and others must *want* the goods (love to possess them) in order to receive them willingly. There must be, therefore, "ownership" in some sense. But the obligation to share goods is powerful—it is *due* the recipients. So it could be argued that various people, by custom, "own a share" in another person's apparent possessions; the possessor does not seem to have outright, full ownership, for if this were so he would have a right to dispose of his property in any way he wished, and this right he clearly does not have. On the other hand, certain items in the possession of an individual are so much his own that they are buried with him when he dies. And there is still another con-founding fact: In no primitive band is anyone denied access to the resources of nature—no individual owns these resources. Apparently, primitive prop-erty is not conceptually simple and homogeneous. It is a complex of rights and duties, and different kinds of things become different kinds of property.

The natural resources on which the bands depend are collective, or com-munal, property in the sense that the territory might be defended by the whole band against encroachment by strangers. Within the band, all families have equal rights to acquire these resources. Moreover, kinsmen in neighbor-ing bands are allowed to hunt and gather at will, at least on request. The most common instance of apparent restriction in rights to resources occurs with respect to nut- or fruit-bearing trees. In some instances, particular trees or clumps of trees are allocated to individual families of the band. This practice is more a division of labor, however, than a division of property, for its purpose seems to be to prevent the waste of time and effort that would occur if several scattered families headed for the same area. It is simpler to conventionalize the allotted use of the several groves, inasmuch as trees are much more permanently located than game or even wild vegetables and grasses. At any rate, even if one family acquired many nuts or fruits and another failed, the rules of sharing would apply so that no one would go hungry.

The things that seem most like private property are those that are made and used by individual persons. Weapons, knives and scrapers, clothing, orna-ments, amulets, and the like, are frequently regarded as private property among hunters and gatherers. Simply because individuals use these items, it would seem obviously disadvantageous, or at best pointless, to have a common store of these kinds of things in any society—even in an imaginary utopia. And, of couse, no definition of communism has ever suggested that such items of personal use must be communalized.

But it could be argued that in primitive society even these personal items are not private property in the true sense. Inasmuch as the possession of such things is dictated by their use, they are functions of the division of labor rather than an ownership of the "means of production." Private ownership of such things is meaningful only if some people possess them and others do not—when, so to speak, an exploitative situation becomes possible. But it is hard to imagine (and impossible to find in ethnographic accounts) a case of some person or persons who, through some accident,

The weapon held by this Pygmy is probably one of the few possessions he will regard as personal property. (C. Trieschmann from
Black Star.)

owned no weapons or clothing and could not borrow or receive such things
from more fortunate kinsmen.

There is an ancient legal term, *personalty*, that is appropriate for items
so closely identified with their use by a particular person. Thus a pet animal,
an ornament, a private magical ritual, a favorite bow, may be regarded as
intensely personal, fully private, but not as private property that is meaningful in terms of creating economic classes, rich and poor, or exploitative relations. A person does not "profit" at the expense of anyone by his possession
of an item of personalty. The closest thing to profit is "credit." People often
claim ownership of something in order to be certain of credit when they lend
it or give it away. *Obligated* to share out the deer he has brought in, the
hunter nevertheless wants it known that it was "his" deer.

If there is no true private property in any useful sense in primitive bands,
are they therefore communistic? The answer, superficially, would seem to
be yes. The answer, more basically and meaningfully, however, is no.

If communism means, simply, the absence of private property in the
resources of nature and in the means of production, then surely hunting-
gathering bands are communistic. But this is at best a superficial state-

24

ment, if not misleading, and it is surely beside the point. Band society is a society based on kinship; it is familistic. But are not families, certainly domestic families in any society, including both "capitalistic America" and "communistic Russia," all equally communistic? If we compare comparables, we find the primitive band of thirty to sixty persons larger, to be sure, than the family in urban America, but it is still a family and it is still a very small-scaled society, as *societies* go. It is not surprising that the members act familistically in economic matters just as in others.

Communism is more meaningfully discussed in the context of its invention as a concept. It was proposed in early modern times as an alternative to capitalism. The units under discussion were large states, usually industrialized. The "public" that either shared ownership or owned private property was the millions of citizens of a state, and it was the state, not a few relatives, that owned (for the public), or did not, the resources of the state. The "instruments of production" that were, or were not, private property were factories, mines, shipping lines, not a stone knife or a few beads. Now private property was something that could be bought and sold, that could affect profit or loss, that functioned, that is, in a market economy, not something that circulated among a few relatives. All this is to say that the usual definitions of communism, and of capitalism for that matter, had an implied, if not explicit, context; they had to do with important property in large, impersonal, complex *states*, not families.

The less superficial, the more meaningful and basic answer must be that the economic nature of primitive bands is not communistic, if the word is to be of any use in discussing types of modern societies. The nature of the primitive economy seems best suggested by the term *familistic*. While it is true that primitive bands and twentieth-century industrial nations are poles apart as types of society, they are not simply opposites or obverse. They are two extremes of an evolutionary spectrum of societies. No modern society, however *communistic*, will ever be *familistic*, as an entire society.

What, then, of the human-nature argument? Is it natural (or unnatural) for human beings to want or need private property, now that we have seen a little something of primitive society? It seems plain enough, as Mr. Cliffe Leslie said, that any people, anywhere, probably have a love of possession (as it seems do most other animals, for that matter). But it is the conduct of the society that we must consider, and this is why the arguments about human nature are so irrelevant. Societies have conducted themselves—or the state or empire has despotically conducted *them*—in a great variety of ways during the course of human history, whereas human nature remains whatever it is (loving its possessions, and so on). When the society is familistic, its economy is familistic. But the economy of a large, complex state is something other than familistic, and the people act in the larger economy as entrepreneurs, or as employees of the state, or whatever.

But not all the time! All societies, no matter how complex, industrialized, even capitalistic, have another economy within the large one. Every person, if he has any family and friends at all, is embedded in a social economy that is familistic and is doing some of the time what our "savage" ancestors did all the time. This primitive behavior of ours is so different from the world of entrepreneurs and the free market that we ordinarily do not even consider it to be a form of economics at all.

Population Regulation

Bands of hunters and gatherers must regulate their numbers in relation to the amount of naturally occurring food resources contained in their territory. Unlike horticulturists, who can intensify crop production in the face of a rising population, hunters and gatherers (by definition) do nothing to control the amount of food available to them. Lee,[27] for example, says that each !Kung band knows how many people can be supported by the territory they exploit, and they consciously regulate themselves so that number is never exceeded. Interestingly, for most hunters and gatherers the maximum number of people in a band territory is only about 30 percent to 40 percent of the amount of people which could be supported during an average year.[28] This phenomenon is best explained by Leibig's Law of the Minimum, which states that populations are regulated by the amount of food available during the worst years. Hunters and gatherers also have a lower limit to their population. In order to adapt to the exigencies of everyday subsistence requirements, the band must be large enough to be a viable economic unit. Since women gather individualistically and men hunt cooperatively, the minimum size of a band is determined by the optimal number of men who can cooperatively hunt. According to G. P. Murdock,[29] the average size of hunting and gathering bands is about thirty people.

Hunters and gatherers have several ways of adapting their numbers during periods of environmental stress. As Lee has shown,[30] the !Kung, in times of plenty, regularly ignore certain edible kinds of food in favor of those they find more delectable. "Iron rations," however, are eaten in times of scarcity when desirable foods are in short supply. Another method for adapting in times of local shortages is for part or all of the band to join a neighboring band in order to share their territory. To do so permission must be gained from the hosts, who will give it only if they feel the additional band can be supported by their land.[31]

Above, we discussed population regulation at the band level, but the

---

[27] R. B. Lee, "!Kung spatial organization." In R. B. Lee and I. Devore, eds. *Kalahari Hunter Gatherers* (Cambridge, Mass.: Harvard University Press, 1977), pp. 74–97.

[28] M. Sahlins, *Stone Age Economics* (Chicago: Aldine, 1972).

[29] "Correlations of exploitive and settlement patterns." In D. Damas, ed., *Contributions to Anthropology: Band Societies*, Bulletin 278, National Museums of Canada, Ottawa (1969), pp. 124–146.

[30] R. B. Lee, *op. cit.*, 1968.

[31] Throughout the Pleistocene the most common method for regulating band size was for part of the band to bud off and occupy an uninhabited territory. But today, since hunters and gatherers are circumscribed by other cultures and geographical barriers, this method is not commonly available.

commonest forms occur at the level of the family and are aimed at controlling either the total number of children in a family or the sex of children. Control at the family level, naturally, has implications for the need for control at the band level. These ends are accomplished through such birth-control practices as periodic abstinence (for example, post-partum sex taboos), infanticide, abortion, contraception, and ethical rules concerning sexual conduct.

Below, we shall discuss why it is important for families to regulate the number and sex of their offspring. Explanations of birth control at the family level in hunter-and-gatherer societies (and indeed for most horticultural groups) have, in the past, focused mainly on the ability of a family to economically support dependents. It was reasoned that hunters and gatherers lived at the brink of starvation and too many nonproductive children could jeopardize the survival of the family. Recent studies [32] show that some hunters and gatherers spend comparatively little time in their food quest, and have no nutritional problems. This realization has led Lee to hypothesize that birth-control practices stem from child transport problems.[33] A great deal of mobility is demanded of !Kung women. They must make long walks to gather food, and treks when the band makes a new camp. The nature of child care is such that they must carry their young children (under the age of four) wherever they go. Lee reasons that a woman can carry but one child at a time and still efficiently accomplish these activities; as a consequence, they space births four years apart so that they need only care for one non-ambulatory child at a time. The wide interval of four years between children is believed by Lee to be accomplished naturally. !Kung females do not reach first menses until quite late in life, between fifteen and seventeen years of age. After menarch they go through a period of post-adolescent sterility, becoming fertile between the ages of eighteen and twenty. The effect of these two factors is to shorten female reproductive span, therefore dampening the rate of population growth for the !Kung as a whole. Finally, !Kung women nurse infants through their third year. It is believed by Lee and his co-workers that this prolonged period of lactation suppresses ovulation.[34] When lactation ceases, fertility returns. Whether this theory is correct for other populations of hunters and gatherers has not been established. But if it is true, it would be a major contribution towards understanding the population dynamics of hunters and gatherers.

W. Denham, contrary to most ethnologists, believes that, in general,

---

[32] Lee *op. cit.*, 1969; Sahlins *op. cit.*, 1968; and Woodburn *op. cit.*, 1968.

[33] R. B. Lee, "Sedentary life among the !Kung Bushmen." In B. Spooner (ed.), *Population Growth: Anthropological Implications*. (Cambridge, Mass.: MIT Press, 1972), pp. 329–342.

[34] N. Howell is investigating this hypothesis among the !Kung. The elements of her theory are as follows: 1) it has been established that ovulation cannot occur if a woman does not have enough body fat; 2) lactating !Kung women require an extra 1,000 kcal/day to make milk; 3) so not enough fat can accumulate on !Kung women while they lactate, causing a suppression of ovulation. "Toward a uniformitarian theory of paleo-demography." *Journal of Human Evolution* 5(1) (1976), 25–40.

population regulation among hunters and gatherers did not occur during the Pleistocene (a period of time covering most human history) and that it is quite exceptional in current populations. Specifically he believes Lee's theory of infant transport and child spacing to be erroneous. In his study [35] of the Alyawara aborigines of Australia he found infant transport to be no problem because there were 1.7 females capable of carrying children per non-ambulatory child; and when women traveled to gathering locales they usually left their infants in camp in the care of someone else. He concluded that infant transport problems do not determine birth-spacing practices, Whether or not birth spacing is a result of problems in child transport is not important. We could also regard it as an adaptive method for: 1) lowering population growth in relation to a non-modifiable supply of food; or 2) insuring the survival of children through investing an adequate amount of time for child care by not spreading too thinly one's effort towards many children (and jeopardizing the survival of all). The important discovery implicit in Lee's and Howell's theory is that fertility in bands may be controlled biologically as well as culturally.[36]

Nearly all hunters and gatherers on which we have reliable information practice infanticide, the killing of the newly born. One rationale behind this act is to control the number of children per family, as described above. Another reason for doing it is to adjust the sex ratio of the population. The adjustment is made in the favor of males, such that more newly born females are killed. The reasons for manipulating the sex ratio in favor of males is first, the rate of population growth in a society is determined mostly by the number of fertile females, and preferential female infanticide is more effective in slowing growth than preferential male infanticide. Second, as demonstrated by C. Schrire and W. L. Steiger,[37] for hunters and gatherers such as the Eskimo who live in marginal areas where starvation and privation are common, female infants are sacrificed because they are not as economically valuable as males—because in the Arctic most of the food is gained by hunting, a task done only by men. Females, since they do not hunt, are regarded as unproductive consumers. Each family desires to have several sons first who can provide food and later be in a position to support the family's daughters. Also, the practices of senilicide (killing the aged) and invalidicide (killing the sick and disabled) are also done by the Eskimos and other marginal groups for the same reasons. The old, sick, and disabled are unproductive, and if fed and cared for could put a serious strain on the group and jeopardize the survival of all.

---

[35] W. Denham, "Population Structure, Infant Transport, and Infanticide among Pleistocene and Modern Hunter-Gatherers," *Journal of Anthropological Research* 30(3) (1974), 191–198.

[36] Lee, *op. cit.*, 1972. Howell, *op. cit.*, 1976.

[37] C. Schrire and W. L. Steiger, "A matter of life and death: an investigation into the practice of female infanticide in the artic." *Man* (NS) 9(2) (1974), 161–184.

Three Society

The people at the band level of social integration make up the smallest as well as the simplest of all human societies. That they stand, therefore, in marked contrast to a modern industrial nation, and live apparently closer to nature because of technological and economic simplicity, may suggest that hunting-gathering bands are in some way closer to ape society than any other. Biologically, the great apes are more like human beings than any other animals. It is therefore natural to think that there are also similarities between ape and human societies, especially when the latter are small and lack the so-called refinements of civilization.

Of course there are some similarities between the social behavior of apes and that of human beings. These are normally the elementary and largely biological and psychological aspects of social life: a mother petting or feeding a baby, the jealousy of siblings, youngsters playing together. But these are common to all levels of human and ape society. If we speak now of culturally determined modes of social behavior, however, we find ourselves on another plane entirely, with no similarity or even farfetched analogy between the social life of apes and that of the simplest hunting-gathering groups.

Subhuman Primate Society

Different species of subhuman primates have different kinds of social organization, but each particular species has its own characteristic type. This is because the social life is set by hereditary biological needs and there are, therefore, very definite limits to the variations in responses that can be induced by different situations and environments. The forms of human society, on the other hand, are tremendously variable in size, complexity, style, and rules of behavior, which demonstrates their adaptability to varying circumstances and environments. This flexibility is possible because human society is structured more by cultural rules and norms than by the biological needs and urges that are common to both apes and humans.

Many normal biological traits, of both apes and humans, are prejudical to social order. The significance of cultural rules and their great power becomes apparent when we notice that at many points these rules create the exact opposite kind of behavior from that which is governed by biological heredity alone. In these respects all human societies are very different from all ape societies; the small rudimentary societies of hunters and gatherers are just as distinct from ape society as are higher societies, and in some respects perhaps more so. Let us take a quick look at a few of these contrasts.

Sexual Behavior. We think of sexual behavior as preeminently biological, probably correctly. And certainly the sex act itself seems similar among both apes and humans, as are apparently the physiological urges that lead to it. But sex is channeled, sublimated, restricted, and tabooed in human society in ways which strikingly modify the social dangers that are inherent in its free manifestation.

Ape society is strongly affected by sex. Many other kinds of animals experience seasonal sexuality only and form families or herds part of the year and are dispersed the rest of it. Ape society is a year-round organization, however, and even though sexual activity may be somewhat seasonal or cyclical between particular pairs, the group association continues.

Sex as practiced by the great apes has both positive and negative effects on group life. The attraction between male and female is, of course, the positive effect and moreover is absolutely basic to society, especially to its continuity. The negative or anti-social aspect of sex is created mostly by male competition in the quest for mates. Ape society is limited in scope and in the kinds of things it can do because this omnipresent disruptive factor is curbed only by the ephemeral victory of one of the contestants. At any given time when there is no actual fighting, therefore, a male despot is ruling over several females and their young, while several other younger or weaker males remain on the fringes of this elementary group.

Food. Apes compete for a limited amount of food, even when they are members of the same horde. Just as they attempt to usurp the females, the strongest animals dominate the taking of food. There is of course one difference: The dominant male (or female dominant over other females) will permit others to eat once he is sated, a privilege not extended to sexual matters. At any rate, individuals compete, and by force or threat of force establish dominance patterns until a complete hierarchy of dominance and submission characterizes the social order of the horde. There is little evidence of friendly sharing or of cooperation among apes except for the collective defense of the group.

Territoriality. The primate horde is a closed social group. Like many other kinds of animals, monkeys and apes (with the possible exception of the mountain gorilla) forage in a territory which they undertake to defend against all competition, and especially against other groups of their own species (because of competition for exactly the same resources). Primates, including humans, are cowardly, though blustering, animals, and do not seem to seek battle for the fun of it. The apes do, however, defend their territories even if mostly with belligerent cries, chest-thumping, or minor skirmishes. The point is that the group, whatever its size, is territorially closed, and this is another significant contrast with human hunting-gathering societies, for even when human societies are strongly territorially based, as we shall see, they are never completely exclusive.

Rudimentary Human Society

Equipped with approximately the same biologically determined urges and needs as apes, human beings at the simplest level of society contrast most strikingly with apes in social behavior because the expression of those urges has been so thoroughly repressed or channeled in the interests of society. Each one of the characteristics of subhuman primates discussed above contrasts with human behavior generally and particularly with the simple hunting-gathering peoples. Humans are able to communicate with one another as no other animal can. Animals do communicate, of course, above all expressing fear, anger, affection, danger, and so on. But in addition to these, human beings learn to create things symbolically that may be purely imaginary; they can create constraints on behavior by communicating cultural rules and taboos, ceremonies and rituals, art and ideology. Thus, despite the considerable biological similarity, in many ways human and subhuman primate behaviors are strikingly and qualitatively distinct. (Chapter Five discusses the human symbolic capacity.)

With respect to sexual behavior, the contrast between apes and humans is apparent in several respects. Most general is the human repression of sex urges in terms of taboos: in all human societies sexual activity is normally private; all regulate exposure of the genitalia in various ways; all limit the age and relationship of partners; and so on. Perhaps the most interesting of all is the so-called incest taboo. All human societies prohibit sexual relations between parents and children, between siblings (except for certain ancient emperors), and in some cases between cousins, or some cousins. This taboo is not always an explicit law or rule, for some peoples simply regard incest as so horrible that they cannot imagine the necessity of having a rule against it. (One of the most interesting things about the incest taboo is the inability of any social scientists or psychologists to explain it— or at least to agree on an explanation.)

Related to the repression and channeling of sex is the institution of marriage. Apes mate, but only humans marry. Marriage is a special kind of pairing arrangement, different from anything found in ape society; it involves social recognition, the acquiescence of society to the arrangement —the opposite of the apes' dominance by threat of force. A marriage, in other words, is in some important sense an *agreement* between groups of people. The agreement, of course, particularly in primitive society, involves a great many matters besides sex. But sexual rights and restrictions are normally included among the others, and for this reason the institution of marriage is one of the more usual of the ways in which sexual urges are modified by cultural rules and taboos. We shall see in later pages that marriage rules have explicit political functions in primitive society, and in this respect sex is often involved directly in peacemaking rather than being the purely disruptive agent that it is in ape society.

Food in primitive society also functions to enhance sociability rather than to be the cause of friction and competition. As we have seen in the preceding chapter, the act of sharing is so frequently a matter of polity as well as etiquette that even when food is scarce and hunger is acute generosity is more likely to prevail over hoarding simply because the maintenance or strengthening of social bonds is so important in rudimentary societies.

In the same way that food is shared in primitive society, so is territory. There are variations in hunting-gathering societies in the degree of territoriality—that is, in the explicitness of boundaries—but in all cases there is some, and in most a rather strict, definition of the band in terms of the general locality it occupies even when boundaries are not specific. But the territory is never occupied exclusively, defended against all outsiders. Normally, the band's territory is closed to strangers and enemies and open to friends and allies. Friends and allies are typically secured by marriages so that eventually they become kinsmen of various kinds and degrees. As we shall see in greater detail in subsequent pages, marriage rules can be created that tie a few bands into even tighter and closer relationships, or they can be so dispersed and attenuated that they include a great many people in the web of kinship. Thus territoriality itself becomes, in human society, variable and adaptable to political situations, only *more or less* closed as environmental-political circumstances require.

In all these points of contrast between human and ape societies it is possible to pinpoint one general characteristic of the apes. Ape society is composed of selfish, "anti-social" beings—an apparent verbal contradiction that reflects a real contradiction. If the positive bonds of attraction are merely sexual, and if many apes are deprived of sex by the dominance of others, then what keeps the society together? Apparently the apes that remain in the horde, even though dominated, do so because of their greater fear of being alone. This may be in some measure a psychobiological deprivation —that apes, like many other animals, seem naturally to require companionship—but it might also be due to real environmental circumstances. S. L. Washburn, an investigator of baboon social life, put it this way: "The troop is a survival mechanism. To not be a social animal is to be a dead animal." Thus the dominance-submission hierarchy, the primate "pecking order," characterizes the social life within the horde and relations among hordes remain antagonistic. A refugee from one group is normally not accepted into another.

Hunting-gathering bands differ more completely from the apes in this matter of dominance than do any other kinds of human society. There is no peck-order based on physical dominance at all, nor is there any superior-inferior ordering based on other sources of power such as wealth, hereditary classes, military or political office. The only consistent supremacy of any kind is that of a person of greater age and wisdom who might lead a ceremony.

Even when individuals possess greater status or prestige than others, the manifestation of the high status and the prerogatives are the opposite of ape-like dominance. Generosity and modesty are required of persons of high status in primitive society, and the rewards they receive are merely the love or attentiveness of others. A man, for example, might be stronger, faster, braver, and more intelligent than any other member of the band. Will he have higher status than the others? Not necessarily. Prestige will be accorded him only if these qualities are put to work in the service of the group—in hunting, let us say—and if he therefore produces more game to give away, and if he does it properly, modestly. Thus, to simplify a bit, greater strength in ape society results in greater dominance, which results in more food and mates and any other things desired by the dominant one; in primitive human society greater strength must be used in the service of the community, and the person, to earn prestige, must literally sacrifice to do so, working harder for less food. As for mates, he ordinarily has but one wife just like the other men.

It seems that the most primitive human societies are at the same time the most egalitarian. This must be related to the fact that because of rudimentary technology this kind of society depends on cooperation more fully more of the time than any other. Apes do not regularly cooperate and share, human beings do—that is the essential difference.

But as some apes became *homo sapiens* and lived in human-like society it was not simply that somehow a gene for altruism overcame the gene for selfishness, thus changing the character of social life. Individual humans are as self-serving as any other animals. The difference lies in the fact that human societies have systems of cultural rewards and punishments and associated joys and fears that can make service to one's fellows become simultaneously a self-service.

The evolution of culture has involved an evolution of technology, and thus an increasing mastery over hostile nature. Just as necessary, just as difficult, but not always so obvious, has been the mastery of man's own nature. The cultural inventions that have enabled societies to become larger, more complex, and stronger all have something to do with remaking or channeling man's biological needs and propensities, most of all with redirecting his selfishness.

Forms of Kinship

The small society of hunters-gatherers is based entirely on kinship. Even when a complete stranger, like an anthropologist, comes to have some kind of consistent social relationship with the band, he should be adopted into it by means of a fictional tie of kinship.

Once Radcliffe-Brown and his native guide approached a strange camp and the guide was unable to establish any bond of kinship, however distant, with anyone in the camp. "That night my 'boy' refused to sleep in the native camp as was his usual custom and on talking to him I found that he was frightened. These men were not his relatives and they were therefore his enemies. This represents the real feeling of the natives on the matter. If I am a blackfellow and meet another blackfellow, that other must be either my relative or my enemy. If he is my enemy I shall take the first opportunity of killing him for fear he will kill me." [1]

In all societies the means by which interpersonal dealings are patterned are statuses of various kinds (the kinds depending on the nature of the society), but in a hunting-gathering society these statuses are nearly exclusively familistic—that is, they are kinship statuses. Hunting-gathering societies are all alike in that their social organization is formed in terms of kinship, although the kinds of kinship patterns vary.

But how can there be different forms of kinship from one society to another? Is not kinship simply genealogy, based on the biology of parenthood? The answer is that we know in fact that there *are* widely differing kinds of kinship—that is, there are varieties of ideological, symbolic ways by which people describe and categorize the people to be considered as relatives. Apes may have mothers and fathers but this is from *our* point of view only —the apes do not know it. On the other hand, many human societies label people mother or father who are not the procreators—a person may have several "mothers." It must be, therefore, that human kinship, the familistic social organization, is not simply genealogy, nor primarily based on the biology of parenthood at all.

(Incidentally, the elementary and apparently simple question of what kinship is and why there can be varieties of kinship systems from one society to another has plagued anthropologists from earliest times. Lewis H. Morgan,

---

[1] A. R. Radcliffe-Brown, "Three Tribes of Western Australia," *Journal of the Royal Anthropological Institute*, Vol. 43 (1913), 150–151.

one of the founders of scientific anthropology, first posed the question and attempted to answer it in a monumental study called *Systems of Consanguinity and Affinity of the Human Family*, published in 1871. But after all that work he was still wrong; that is, his ideas are not accepted today, nor is any other theory widely accepted. This could be taken as a simple measure of the immaturity of anthropology, for surely the problem must be soluble.)

The different kinds of band organization and related systems of kinship nomenclature among hunters-gatherers have been divided into two major types: the *patrilocal band* and the *composite band*,[2] with some intermediate cases, of course.

The patrilocal type of band organization is created by two related rules or customs pertaining to marriage. First is *band exogamy:* one marries someone from outside one's own band. Second is *virilocal marital residence:* the married couple join the man's band, not the woman's (which would be *uxorilocal residence* in anthropological parlance). Virilocality results in patrilocality: that is, children grow up in their father's band, not in the mother's original band. The band is thus also patrilineal; the members are all related through the male line because of the residence rule. But this is from our point of view; we understand it this way because we are accustomed to reckoning descent, even the pedigrees of dogs and horses. But hunting-gathering peoples do not normally do this, and the composition of the band is understood by them as being formed by the residence rule; hence patrilocal is a better name for the arrangement than patrilineal.

An interesting fact related to the above point is that some primitive peoples —the native Australians particularly—do not recognize the role of the father in procreation. One of the ancestral spirits that lives in the locality is responsible for inducing the pregnancy, thus the child is in part a reincarnation of some unspecified ancestor. We need not argue about whether the people *really* do or do not know about the relation of sexual intercourse to pregnancy. It is easily conceivable that they do not—the relationship is certainly not obvious—but the point is that "real" paternity is not relevant to the way the society is ordered. A person is a member of the band he is born into, and the band is in a place. It turns out to be the father's band and place because that is where the married couple lives. But what does the word "father" mean if father's paternity is not comprehended? The answer is easy: the father is the husband of the mother (an answer, incidentally, that is also found in the *Code Napoléon*).

The composite band, on the other hand, does not follow regularized customs of band exogamy and marital residence. The band as a whole has a rather amorphous structure—neither consistently patrilocal nor matrilocal— and lacks the affinal kinship relationship that is regularized in some other

---

[2] See Julian H. Steward, *Theory of Culture Change* (Urbana: University of Illinois Press, 1955), Chaps. 7 and 8. Steward was the first to describe these types. He called the patrilocal band type *patrilineal,* but the change to patrilocal was made here for reasons which will emerge.

particular bands. "Composite" is a good name for this kind of band, because it seems to have been formed by the agglomeration of unrelated peoples after the catastrophic effects of contact with modern civilization. In many cases native peoples had no resistance to foreign diseases and were nearly wiped out and also were frequently forced to migrate to new areas as refugees. A usual consequence of either of these situations—and they often occurred simultaneously—was the formation of a composite group, sometimes quite large, out of the remnants of the bands. The nuclear families and the groups formed of brothers and their families tend to arrange marriages and the place of post-nuptial residence for expedient reasons of their own, without reference to group polity.

But if patrilocality is usual for hunting-gathering bands and if it is due to the virilocal residence rule, then the question naturally emerges: Why virilocality? And inasmuch as band exogamy is presupposed, we also wonder about that: Why exogamy? It is another of those deceptively simple questions, like that of the incest taboo, but in this case we seem to have the answer better in hand.

Let us first be clear about one thing that has caused considerable confusion in anthropological discussions of both exogamy and the incest taboo. Exogamy is a kind of rule about *marriage*, not just sexual behavior. The incest taboo has to do with *sexual behavior*, not marriage. Our own tendency to connect marriage with sex—as we do in our ideals, at least—is a very peculiar association that grew up in our very unusual society. In primitive society particularly, and in most societies generally, marriage is undertaken for a great many reasons, but "love" is irrelevant and sexual rights are almost incidental to it —in fact, in many societies the married couple might never have met, in others they may have been betrothed before they were born (promised by the parents).

Why *do* people in primitive societies marry? For one thing, people seem to want to establish themselves as adults, and there is no way to do this except by marriage. The economic division of labor in hunting-gathering societies is such that unless adult males and females share the work as husband and wife, each would remain a dependent, an appendage of another family—ordinarily that of their parents. Marriage is an economic necessity, as we have seen in the preceding chapter, whereas sex, however much a necessity, is easily satisfied in primitive society without marriage. But there are probably many other adult requirements that marriage does satisfy. Probably most people want children, others want to get away from their own parents or siblings, and so on. But all these are only reasons why various individuals might find the institution of marrige welcome, not why the institution exists in the first place, nor what its role is for the society as a whole.

In primitive society a certain kind of marriage rule results in a certain kind of system of relationship. Marriage is an economic institution from the point of view of the partners, perhaps, but for the parents of the couple, and especially for the band as a whole, marriage has very important *political* functions. The variations in the marriage rule have various political results, particularly with respect to the alliances created among bands, and they can be narrow and firm or extended and loose.

It seems obvious that the reason why the various rules of marriage are all different forms of exogamy is related to the matter of political alliance. It is frequently stated this way by the primitive peoples themselves, as well as being an obvious conclusion we might come to from witnessing its function. An early anthropologist, E. B. Tylor, put it this way:

> Among tribes of low culture there is but one means known of keeping up permanent alliance, and that means is intermarriage. . . . Again and again in the word's history, savage tribes must have had plainly before their minds the simple practical alternative between marrying-out and being killed-out. Even far on in culture, the political value of inter-marriage remains. . . . "Then we will give our daughters unto you, and we will take your daughters to us, and we will dwell with you and we will become one people," is a well-known passage of Israelite history.[3]

That the marriage rule is a political device for the society rather than merely a convenience for the individuals is illustrated by the wide prevalence of two institutions closely related to it. These are the so-called *levirate* and *sororate*, which preserve a marriage arrangement even after the death of one of the partners. The levirate is the rule that obligates a man to marry the widow in case of the death of his brother. (*Levir* means "husband's brother" in Latin. The levirate was practiced by the ancient Hebrews [Deuteronomy XXV: 5–20].) The sororate obligates a woman to marry the widower in case of the death of her sister. These are not merely reflections of the inclinations of individuals, clearly, for they are *rules*, widespread in primitive society, imposed on individuals by the society.

Exogamy, then, is comprehensible as a rule of marriage made by a group, and its function is to widen the network of kinship relations. And like typical political regulations it is explicitly end-oriented, consciously and intentionally. Endogamic (marrying *in*) restrictions are not usually so explicit, often being nothing more than a vague feeling on the part of individuals that they should not marry people too strange or distant, for they would not make good allies or adapt easily as family members. The latent function of endogamic restrictions would be, of course, to prevent the group of relatives from becoming too large and the kinship ties of alliance too attenuated. But mostly, primitive peoples have a rule of marriage that states that the specific group (or kinship category) must exchange marriage partners; the rule thus has simultaneous exogamic and endogamic aspects.

But why are the rules so often rigid about where the married couple should reside, and why, above all, should it be the husband's locality? A usual first-thought on this subject by anthropologists has been that in hunting-gathering societies the economic significance of the male's hunting is so great

---

[3] E. B. Tylor, "On a Method of Investigating the Development of Institutions: Applied to Laws of Marriage and Descent," *Journal of the [Royal] Anthropological Institute*, Vol. 18 (1888), 245–269.

and his knowledge of his own territory is so important that he must stay in his own region. There are two things wrong with this idea, however.

One is that there is great variation in different societies in the economic significance of the males' activities. The Eskimo, for example, subsist nearly exclusively on the male hunters' catch, the only exception being the occasional fishing the women might do. The Yahgan of Tierra del Fuego, on the other hand, subsist mostly on the shellfish gathered exclusively by women. But if anything, the Yahgan have been more consistently given to virilocality than the Eskimo. In our sample of bands there is not, in fact, any correspondence between the significance of hunting and the strictness of virilocality.

The second difficulty is that while it may be true that hunters need to know their terrain, it is rare that they would not be equally familiar with the terrain of the neighboring bands that they would be likely to marry into. The band's "country" is normally set by the circuit of moves of the camps in their search for vegetable foods, whereas hunters go where the game leads them, except too deeply into territory that is clearly of enemies.

It seems likely that the importance of the cooperation of males in hunting and in warfare is a more significant factor. To hunt many of the animals, especially those in large herds, requires close collaboration of several men, just as does warfare. The women's gathering activities, whatever their economic significance to the society, ordinarily do not require the delicate coordination of several people. Thus women could be lost to their own band when they marry, and others gained, without weakening it so much as it would be by breaking up the teams of brothers and male cousins who grew up together.

A much simpler explanation has sometimes been offered. Women are the "gifts" from one band to another, exchanged reciprocally as a form of alliance-making, simply because males are so dominant in hunting-gathering society—*they* make the rules. There are societies that are uxorilocal, however, but males are still dominant, still make the rules. These are horticultural societies and the gardening is done by women, and much of it is collaborative as well.

The virilocal-patrilocal band, at any rate, is the usual form of band society. It also has a typical marriage rule that anthropologists call cross-cousin marriage. Any kin group that is exogamous and of sufficient size to include cousins can have only half of the possible cousins, so-called *parallel cousins*, while the other cousins, the *cross-cousins*, are found in the group or groups which have intermarried with this group. In Fig. 1, which illustrates this rule, the cross-cousins are blacked out.

The parallel cousins, it is evident, are the children of Ego's aunts and uncles who, because of exogamy and the rule of residence, are likely to have remained in the band (*e.g.*, the father's brother) or to have come into it on marriage (*e.g.*, the mother's sister). The cross-cousins are the children of the aunts and uncles who have left the band after marriage (the father's sisters) or who were born away and remain there because of the rule of residence (the mother's brothers). This rule of marriage is the simplest, involving only two groups—conceptually, at least. More than two bands may

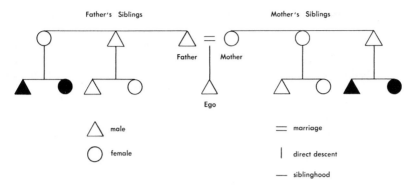

Figure 1

be involved, actually, but there is a frequent tendency to form a dual organization, or *moiety*, as it is called in anthropology, arranging the several bands into two intermarrying sides.

There are a few instances of special permutations. Some Australian groups (the Northern Arunta are the best-known example) have a rule of second cross-cousin marriage—*i.e.*, one marries into the category of a mother's mother's brother's daughter's daughter rather than that of mother's brother's daughter. This rule has the effect of broadening greatly the network of relatives. One cannot marry into the mother's group but must marry into mother's cross-cousin's group. Twice as many relatives are harvested this way but, of course, the relationships are only half as close.

A few Australian groups prescribe a form of cross-cousin marriage that anthropologists call *matrilateral cross-cousin marriage*. Ego must marry a cross-cousin from mother's group (*i.e.*, the category mother's brother's daughter) but cannot marry any of the other cross-cousins, the patrilateral (*i.e.*, father's sister's daughter). This rule results in a given band giving wives to one group and receiving them from another—at least three, usually more, therefore must be involved.

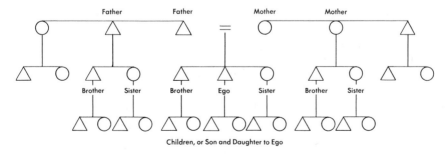

Figure 2

Related to the rules of marriage and residence are differences in the ways in which the kinsmen are categorized. The most common is the kind usually called the *bifurcate-merging system.* This categorization is closely associated with the cross-cousin marriage rule and moiety system, as can be easily suggested by taking the same diagram used in Fig. 1 to show cross-cousins and adding the bifurcate-merging terms of kinship to it.

From our own pedigree-conscious point of view the bifurcate-merging system is most curious. How can a person have several fathers and, above all, several *mothers*? How can certain cousins (the parallels) be "confused" with one's own brothers and sisters? The answer must be that people certainly will not really confuse their own siblings with cousins or their own mother with some other woman, so perhaps the questions are not being asked in the appropriate form. Let us assume for the moment that the people are not trying to state genealogical lines, but instead merely take a look at the social world of a member of a patrilocal band and see what categories of persons actually exist. These social categories we may call statuses, not meaning anything more special by this than that the category has to do with appropriate forms of interpersonal conduct. By leaving this definition so general and vague we avoid deciding in advance whether any particular terms are or are not genealogical. Any status in any given society *could* be genealogical, or based on strength, wealth, political office, skin color, or anything. We are thus permitted to investigate more freely.

But *this* we know for certain, without any argument: Whether a person is a male or female is a universally recognized and very important criterion of status. There is probably no need to discuss this point except to mention that whereas all societies recognize this set of related statuses, some give it much more significance in the etiquette of behavior than others. One of the characterstics of the urban U.S.A. and of modern cities in general is the considerable economic emancipation of women compared to older types of society, more social equality with men, and a much freer kind of social inter-action—the statuses are more equal and therefore somewhat diminished in significance. But down the evolutionary scale the sex differentiation apparently increases. This conclusion is suggested, anyway, by the strictness and completeness of the division of labor by sex in a hunting-gathering society.

Another important social division is along the lines of generations. And again the significance of generational status and of age generally, like the sexual distinction, seems to be much more pronounced in primitive societies than in our own.

A third distinction involves affines. The kinship world of any person falls into two categories: "own" family group and "in-law" family group. In a patrilocal band this distinction corresponds to the difference between father's relatives and mother's relatives. Genealogically, both kinds of relatives are equally related to Ego, the individual. But they are not socially equal from Ego's point-of-view because of territoriality and exogamy. Father's group is his "own" group, the intimate one; mother's own kin are the "others," those actual and potential in-laws with whom more careful, restrained, formal kinds of conduct are the rule.

In all societies one behaves differently toward a brother-in-law than toward a brother, differently toward a mother-in-law than toward a mother. But just as in the case of sex and generational standing this status distinction between affinal moieties is more important in the more primitive societies. It is also much more broadly based, more highly generalized, in a society of patrilocal bands, in the sense that Ego conducts himself as a "brother-in-law" toward all males of his own generation in the *other* moiety or band of whatever the category he will marry into. This is the rule with all the other basic categories, as well.

In essence, then, the bifurcate-merging kinship system is a nomenclature for only four kinds of social persons, each kind further subdivided by sex. These four basic categories are as follows: adjacent generation in own group, adjacent generation in affinal group, own generation in own group, own generation in affinal group. In genealogical terms we would discover that such people as mother's brother's children belong in the last-named category, father's brother's children in the third, mother's brother in the second, father's brother in the first, and so forth. Remember, however, that this is *our* way of looking at the matter, because we are much more inclined to distinguish individual genealogical categories than are most primitive peoples.

The above kind of system seems to be standard among relatively undisturbed patrilocal bands. But not all the hunting-gathering peoples of the world were undisturbed at the time they were described. In some instances, modern influences, such as depopulation and the subsequent agglomeration of unrelated peoples, have caused the composite, unstructured band—which is to say, bands that do not exhibit group affinity.

Certain Eskimo villages offer a good example of one of the prevalent forms of composite organization, with a kinship terminological pattern that seems related to it. In most respects this terminology resembles the kinship system of the United States. This is related to the fact that the individual household of relatives, the nuclear family, is set apart from other relatives as a residential group. This means that Ego's brothers and sisters are terminologically distinct from all the cousins, and these cousins are not divided into cross and parallel categories.

Some of the Paiute Indians of the American Southwest illustrate another terminological pattern which itself seems to have resulted from, or at least to be related to, the lack of clear-cut band affinality or moiety distinctions. This is the so-called *generational system*. Ego's relatives in any generation

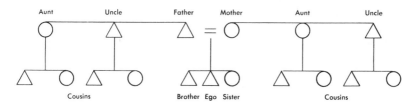

Figure 3

are subdivided only in terms of sex—that is, no distinction is made between siblings and cousins, nor between mother's and father's siblings from others of that generation.

The Pygmy inhabitants of the Andaman Islands present an interesting case. These people live in territorial bands of a sort, but they are not clearly exogamous, with reciprocal marriage relations between specific bands, know nothing of moiety, and practice no clear-cut patrilocality. The Andamanese terminological pattern varies depending on whether the terms are being used in address or in reference. The terms used in address are simply status terms of respect and all they mean, apparently, is "older age" or "upper generation." This seems to be like our own usage of "sir" and "madam." Sometimes, also as in our own usage, this term is used along with a person's name. Other persons equal or lesser in status to Ego may be addressed directly by name alone. The Andamanese terms of reference—that is, the way in which they may refer to their relationship to another person who is not present—is similar to the Eskimo practice we described earlier of isolating the individual nuclear family or household from other relatives in each generation.

Kinship Groups

Although the band society of hunters-gatherers is the simplest and smallest of the various human social levels, it does contain discernible groups and categories. The subgroupings, of course, include the usual nuclear family of father, mother, and children. Above the level of the nuclear family, but smaller than the band itself, there is usually another discernible group that anthropologists call the *extended family*. It is sometimes an actual residential group, sometimes not, but in most cases it is a grouping of families that will remain together more often than with others in the band. In both the patrilocal and composite type of band, the extended family is typically the *patrilateral* extended family, which means simply that brothers, and the families of these brothers, are more apt to range a given area contiguously or at least to meet one another more often than they meet other people. They camp close together whenever possible and the brothers frequently collaborate in hunting.

The band itself, of course, is the next higher level of agglomeration and then, as already indicated, above that there may be bands, usually several, often arranged as "sides" of a moiety arrangement. Because of the tendency of certain bands to intermarry more than with some others, they will become somewhat distinct politically from other neighbors.

So far we have been talking about demographic units that can be quite variable, depending on the form of ecological adaptation of the society. In some cases, as, for example, when whaling used to be practiced by the Eskimo, many people might reside together for entire summers, but disperse during the winter for the seal hunts. Or the hunting-gathering peoples of the Great Basin of Nevada might roam as widely separated families most of the time,

Structure built for kayaks and for storing seal meat to protect them from the dogs. The Eskimos are the only hunting-gathering people with no limitations on their hunting activities because of food storage problems. (Culver Pictures.)

but after the pine nut harvest large numbers of people might congregate in one place for the winter.

There is another kind of social unit that needs to be distinguished from residential groups. These are forms of association, familiar to us at all levels of society, that we may call *sodalities*. Sodalities are social forms that have been created purposefully in order to accomplish something. A group of men, for example, might form an organization in order to conduct certain kinds of magical ceremonies. Or women might meet regularly to play some kind of gambling game. Inasmuch as such associations are not true residential groups, being only infrequently agglomerated at best, they are not such natural-seeming, visible units as are the family, extended family, or even the band itself. They therefore need some signs that will denote membership and make it more meaningful. These are ordinarily kinds of insignia or body decorations and frequently a repertoire of special songs, ceremonies, and so on.

Since sodalities are not residential units, their membership will tend to intersect the membership of residential groups. This has the effect, whether intended or not by the members, of making for better social relations among the separate residential units. It can also have some straightforward political

43

functions as a consequence of its nonlocal character, for troubled relations between residential groups can be arbitrated by members of the groups who belong to the same sodality.

We have mentioned that sodalities emphasize such things as insignia, ceremonies, songs, and secret rituals in order to make themselves appear more like a true group. Now it should be apparent that a residential group itself could use such things in order to make the group more solid. It would seem, then, that any band society that is widely scattered most of the time—that is, when the residential factor in the association of the families is weak—would therefore be more likely to add sodality-like characteristics to their society. This is true in several instances, and strikingly so for the inhabitants of the interior deserts of Australia, who are, perforce, those who are widely scattered in their subsistence activities most of the time.

Some of the cultural features used to enhance sociality in band societies are universal and obvious. Bands have names and name the territories they inhabit, even if the members are widely scattered. And when the boundaries are not discernible, the bands still tend to name local centers by which they are characterized. All bands indulge in some kinds of distinctive ceremony. Sometimes the ceremonials are only for individuals, but if a band as a whole gets together for the purpose, then its solidarity increases. Ceremony and ritual of course all have an obvious sociological function, whether intended or not, as well as ideological and psychological bases. But there is one kind of ceremony and associated belief that seems so explicitly and so primarily related to social integration that it should be given a little more prominence at this point. This is the widespread institution called *totemism*.

A totem is a species of animal, plant, or sometimes some other aspect of nature that is conceived to be in a mystical social relationship with the members of a group. Among the Algonkian-speakers of North America and the natives of Australia the totem (an Algonkian word) is ancestral to a particular kinship group. Thus groups are named "Crow," "Hawk," "Wallaby," and so on, by virtue of this kinship to the species. In central Australia nearly every group and category of persons is distinguished by its totemic name and the rituals it conducts with respect to the totem.

One of the most interesting characteristics of totemism is the kind of ceremony called "rites of increase." Each totemic group is responsible for the ceremony that insures the continuity and well-being of its totemic animal or plant species. These ceremonies may be very elaborate and take several days, and some of the more important ones attract large numbers of people. The increase ceremonies differ greatly from one another in detail, but they all have the following features. (1) The heart of the ceremony is a very detailed, secret ritual performance by the members of the totemic group which is supposed to insure that the particular plant or animal species will multiply. (2) Next there is a sort of communion service in which the ceremonial leader publicly tastes a bit of the totem. (3) Then the members of the totemic group taste a bit of it. (They cannot eat their totem except in such rituals.) (4) The assembled people then feast freely upon the totem.

Inasmuch as the participants believe that such ceremonies are necessary to insure the well-being of the various species, every totemic group has a role in the survival of all the others. Thus a ceremonial division of labor exists which, like its economic counterpart, promotes an organismic solidarity among the groups.[4]

Just as religion in the form of totemism is difficult to separate from social aspects of life in band society, so it is with other cultural institutions. As we saw in the first chapter, economic exchange is as social as it is utilitarian and there are no purely economic institutions such as markets. Perhaps the most surprising thing, however, is the absence of political organization. How are group relations regulated? How is anti-social conduct within the groups controlled? How are quarrels adjudicated? Who is in charge? So far we have sketched the outlines of the social order of band society but have not discussed a major problem of the society, how it is *kept* in order. This problem and the means for solving it is the subject of the next chapter.

---

[4] This was essentially the point made by Radcliffe-Brown in 1929, in "The Sociological Theory of Totemism," *Proceedings of the Fourth Pacific Science Congress* (Java, Batavia, 1930). Lévi-Strauss plays down the above rather utilitarian perspective in the favor of the view of the classificatory homology between social groupings and relations in the natural world and the cultural. Claude Lévi-Strauss, *Totemism*, trans. Rodney Needham (Boston: Beacon Press, 1963).

Four *Polity*

Any society, no matter how elementary, is more than an aggregation of individuals. It is an organization. We have seen some of the ways in which society is structured and the ways in which an individual's behavior is patterned by rules of etiquette, statuses with appropriate role expectations, customs of marriage, and so on. These are important features that all societies must emphasize if they are to function at all. But not all people are the same, and no society is ever able to socialize perfectly all its members. More important, no society is ever able to synchronize perfectly the action of groups with respect to one another. Diversity and conflict are certainly usual aspects of the human condition, so much so that a basic question in any general consideration of society is: What holds it together?

We are talking about something now that is above, or additional to, socialization—social control by regulation. *Polity* in the meaning used in this chapter refers simply to the matter of regulation, the preserving of social order by means of some kind of authority. The problems of the social order are of two basic kinds: the control of deviant behavior and the direct-

46

ing of concerted actions. Deviant behavior may involve many kinds of difficulties for a society, but most critical are what we would call crimes or torts in our own society, so gross a violation of standards that others are physically, socially, or economically injured. In primitives societies the greatest difficulty arises when such injuries are inflicted by persons from one group on those from another. The direction of concerted action also is most difficult when more than one social group is involved, for otherwise the statuses built into the kinship system of a single group can serve as regulatory, decision-making devices. At any rate, every society finds it necessary to reach decisions that are binding on a number of people above the level of the domestic family, and every society has to be able to resolve discords between families. Thus every society not only has ways in which people are positively rewarded for behaving appropriately but who are also in some way or another punished for disobeying the rules.

Authority of course, like charity, begins in the home. Everyone in the world knows how young people are subordinated to adults and how disciplinary action and systems of rewards are used by adults to bring children into conformity with the necessities and expectations of the family, as well as of the broader society. But so usual in the world is this system of authority based on the statuses of father and mother, elder brother and sister, and so on, that in a discussion of kinds of societies, there is little use in talking about the system of internal governing of families themselves. That is the family social system, not polity. What we ordinarily mean by governing, polity, authority, in a comparative social study refers to the problems of the relations of individuals who are not in the same domestic unit and who are outside the forms of authority that exist within it. These are the problems, then, that cannot be solved by the mere sex and age status differentiations of a nuclear family. They are problems that arise from the difficulties of coordination or of dissension between families, between bands, and between independent societies. And these problems of course are the most difficult ones; the more remote the relationship of the individual groups, the more difficult is the process of arriving at decisions and of punishing deviant behavior, and above all, of adjudicating the difficulties that arise in relations among the groups.

The Uses of Authority

Authority may resort to three basic techinques in controlling deviancy and in synchronizing group actions: reinforcement, administration, and adjudication.[1] *Reinforcement* is the use of authority to prevent deviations from culturally prescribed behavior. It is the attempt to insure the continuity of established codes and thus restrict the kinds of behavior that threaten the social order. Reinforcement can be many kinds of things: It

[1] Walter Goldschmidt, *Man's Way* (New York: Holt, Rinehart and Winston, 1959), p. 92.

can be simply admonitions by an elder to a young man and the preaching of ethics; or it can range from the action of a criminal court to a teacher giving poor marks for deportment. *Administration* is the use of authority in directing the concerted action of people: getting people to go hunting at a certain time or a certain place, or directing a ceremony, summoning people for a feast, or calling the turns at a square dance. *Adjudication* is the familiar use of authority in resolving conflict between people or groups. Let us consider these three roles in more detail as they are applied in hunting-gathering societies.

Reinforcement.   Much of the control of social behavior is achieved merely in terms of custom. Regularities, uniformities, and continuities, particularly in the realm of etiquette, have a great deal to do with the integration of society. Reinforcing standards of behavior such as habitual etiquette through family training is extremely important. But now we are talking about reinforcement by authoritative means, not the acquisition of habits in childhood within the family. If every person born into a social system were completely molded by education and training, thoroughly socialized, and fitted into a thoroughly homogeneous culture, then there would be no internal social problems because each individual would be adjusted precisely to the system. But we know that there is no unambiguous system of culture and that no individual is so thoroughly socialized. At some point or another the problem of reinforcing generally accepted standards of behavior always comes down to a matter of authority.

All systems of reinforcement by authority rest on some accepted uses of punishment. These we shall call *sanctions*. Sanction is a much broader term than law, and may be taken to include law. Nevertheless, in hunting-gathering societies formal systems of law do not exist, nor, of course, does the state which would enforce the formal code. But sanctioned forms of deterrence do, and they can vary all the way from punishments like ostracism, ridicule, and withdrawal of privilege, to actual physical violence, even death.

Understand first that in primitive societies the sanctions against any breach of etiquette are ordinarily not a consequence of an authoritative *person's* action. The usual reaction to a breach of etiquette is merely a general withdrawal from the culprit, depriving him of the courtesy to which he would normally have been entitled. In extreme cases, ostracism has been invoked. In any small society etiquette is a potent form of social regulation because all social relations are of the face-to-face sort. No one can escape consequences for a breach of etiquette, whereas it may be possible to conceal a crime. This is to say that the sanctions of a breach of etiquette in small groups are punishment by society itself, the community as a whole.

But what of the true delinquent, the person who is chronically anti-social, the bully, the thief, the habitual liar? The normal sanctions of the society or community as a whole—gossip, ridicule, withdrawal, and so on—fail to have any influence on this kind of deviant because he is powerful enough to go it alone, contemptuous of gossip, perhaps insane. There is of course no formal means of procedure because there is no government and no law and thus no standardization of how society is to punish any person for any particular misdemeanor or crime. But a person who so consistently misbehaves, particularly if his behavior harms groups other than his own, will ultimately draw his own group against him simply because he is endangering them all. It has happened in hunting-gathering societies that a person's own band, including his own family, may plot to remove him. In such a case it is usual that the person chosen to do away with the malefactor will be a close relative, if possible, for then the murder can lead to no further revenge—a family will not proceed against itself.

To the extent that reinforcement is a function of the authority of particular persons in band society, it is extremely informal and is largely a matter of the social status that a man holds. The most usual status and the most usual use of it in the role of reinforcement is simply that of admonition by an elder to a younger. This of course is standard in the family, older brother over younger, father over son, and so on. It seems, however, that in multi-family communities in general the status "elder" is more significant in the context of reinforcement toward conformity than any other. Men are generally accorded greater respect in this context than females, also, possibly because men are ordinarily occupied in more political-like situations outside the family circle than are women. So we may say in summary that in band societies the elder males have a more authoritative position than do others.

In all societies adults are held to be superior to children, and this is so natural as to hardly require explanation. In a primitive society old men would be held to be superior to younger adult men for exactly the same reason—the possession of greater experience and wisdom. This latter point might seem a little peculiar to us, for one of the characteristics of our society is that aged persons have become "old-fashioned," unable to cope with changing circumstances as well as younger people. They may be respected but it is often a rather nominal respect. But this is precisely not the case in a stable primitive society. In a society that is not developing or changing, particularly one that is not undergoing complex industrial change, the older a person becomes the more he knows about life. The problems of adapting to and living in a given environment are the same for all living generations at any given time, just as they were for the forefathers, in a band-like society. It follows that since the society has remained relatively unchanged for millennia, then older men know better about how things are to be done, and thus it is of advantage to accord them respect and above all to heed their advice. And here we should be reminded that advice and admonition about social and ritual behavior are equally as important as advice and admonition about hunting or gathering.[2]

---

[2] This situation of course becomes drastically changed when a primitive society becomes subjected to modern influences and when there is an opportunity for some of the people to adapt themselves to European culture, for example. Then there is a likelihood that young-old factionalism will set in, the elders striving to maintain the ways of the society, the youths struggling to embrace the new ways of the alien world.

Administration. Administration is the role authority assumes with respect to problems of concerted group action. It is what we ordinarily mean by the word "leadership." The necessities for administration of group action and close coordination are varied and numerous in hunting-gathering societies. They would include such usual things as camp movements, a collaborative hunting drive, and particularly any kind of skirmishing with enemies. But despite the obvious significance of leadership in such activities, a hunting-gathering society is, as in other matters, distinctive in that it has no formal leadership of the sort that we see in later stages of cultural development. There is no permanent office of headman; leadership moves from one person to another depending on the type of activity that is being planned. For example, one very old man might be the favorite for planning a ceremony because of his great ritual knowledge, but another person, younger and more skilled at hunting, might be the normal leader of the hunting party.

Above all, there is no leader or headman in the sense usually associated with the word *chief.* "Bossiness" is not tolerated, and humility, as in other contexts, is valued. Anyone in authority in any particular endeavor is clearly there with the consent of the governed, so to speak. As Meggitt once put it with reference to Australian elders, "Whatever *de facto* control they had over the actions of others simply derived from their ability to make suggestions based on first-hand knowledge of commonly-occurring situations. . . ." He went on to say, ". . . a man attracted social prestige only as long as he could validate his status by actual performance." [3] The most certain thing we can say is that in this matter of leadership of group activities the leader is a man of experience and skill. But a man's skill ordinarily tends to vary from one activity to another—thus leaders vary.

Some people like to lead, of course. But as we have mentioned in other contexts, a primitive society of hunting-gathering bands is exceptionally egalitarian. People cannot seek leadership, honor, or prestige but should stay within the role prescribed by their status within the kinship system.

> The nature of the [kinship] . . . roles which are played by every Yir Yoront means that every individual relationship between males involves a definite and accepted inferiority or superiority. A man has no dealing with another man (or with women, either) on exactly equal terms. And where each is at the same time in relatively weak positions and in an equal number of relatively strong positions, no one can be either absolutely strong or absolutely weak. A hierarchy of a pyramidal or inverted-Y type to include all the men in the system is an impossibility. Without a radical change in the entire kinship structure, the Yir Yoront cannot even tolerate mild chiefs or headmen, while a leader with absolute authority over the whole group would be unthinkable.[4]

---

[3] M. J. Meggitt, *Desert People* (Chicago: The University of Chicago Press, 1960), p. 250.

[4] R. L. Sharp, "People Without Politics," *Systems of Political Control and Bureaucracy in Human Societies,* ed. Verne E. Ray (Seattle: American Ethnological Society, 1958), p. 5. Also in Bobbs-Merrill Reprint Series.

It is possible at any given time that there may be a person who combines knowledge and skill in such a variety of activities that he may be more influential than anyone else in the band. This appearance of full leadership, however, is only informal, and one which is best called *charismatic*—depending on the capabilities of the person and not a formal office. There is obviously no election or means of selection of such a headman; a man having the characteristics of a good leader simply becomes more and more respected until he seems to be *the* leader. A charismatic leader's influence is the sort that would perhaps be best called moral. He must be a respected person, one whose advice is sought and heeded, rather than one who commands. Perhaps the best characterization of the type of leadership in band society is represented by the title, *Isumatag*, given the headman by some of the Arctic Eskimo, which means "he who thinks." This is to say that leadership is essentially an advisory, not executive, authority, in this kind of society.

Radcliffe-Brown says of the Pygmies of the Andaman Islands:

> Besides the respect for seniority there is another important factor in the regulation of the social life, namely the respect for certain personal qualities. These qualities are skill in hunting and in warfare, generosity and kindness, and freedom from bad temper. A man possessing them inevitably acquires a position of influence in the community. His opinion on any subject carries more weight than another even older man. The younger men attach themselves to him, are anxious to please him by giving him any presents that they can, or by helping him in such work as carving a canoe, and to join him in hunting parties or turtle expeditions. . . .
>
> There was no special word to denote such men and distinguish them from others. In the languages of the North Andaman they were spoken of as *er-kuro* = "Big." [5]

It is noteworthy that in this passage Radcliffe-Brown used the word "influence." This is probably a better word than "authority" to suggest the social role of persons of high prestige. Authority suggests some position in a hierarchical order. But clearly none of these so-called leaders hold consistent positions of authority, nor do they exercise their influence in an authoritarian manner. Elizabeth Thomas, in describing the South African Bushmen, mentions an important man named Toma who had apparently won his high status over two others who had expected to hold it.

> But neither ever contested Toma's position as leader, for it was not a position which Toma held with force or pressure but simply by his wisdom and ability, and people prospered under him. No Bushman wants prominence, but Toma went further than most in avoiding prominence, he had almost no possessions and gave away everything that came into his hands. He was diplomatic, for in exchange for his self-imposed poverty he won the respect and following of all the people there. He enjoyed his position, and, being strangely free from the normal

---

[5] A. R. Radcliffe-Brown, *The Andaman Islanders* (Glencoe, Ill.: The Free Press, 1948), p. 45.

strains and jealousies of Bushmen, he saw justice clearly and hence he led his people well.[6]

The above characteristic of Bushmen leaders is essentially the same as those of other hunting-gathering societies elsewhere. We may fittingly end the discussion with the following apt summary statement of leadership among the hunting Indians of northwestern Canada:

> In sum, the leader characteristically has a very tenuous position in Northeastern Athabascan society. He might serve as adviser, coordinator, director and perhaps initiator of specific military actions and/or of occasional and particular economic activities beyond the day-to-day hunting and snaring routine. Also, by virtue of his prestige, gained from his superior abilities and his awe-inspiring powers, he might act as the prime opinion-giver in social matters within the band. His "authority" lay in putting his stamp of approval upon decisions or viewpoints arrived at by the group as a whole or, more specifically, his male peers. The wise chief or leader had his finger upon the pulse of individual and group opinions. He had to woo others to his way of thinking or, that failing, to alter his course accordingly. His position might be buttressed by the attribution of powerful medicine and by the Europeans' evaluation and use as "trading chief" of his already dominant role. But the power of a strong or "great" leader lay in his influence rather than his "legal" authority. Ordinarily he had neither the moral nor physical resources to impose his will. Birket-Smith's characterization of the Chipewyan chief as *primus inter pares* keynotes the position of the Northern Dené leader.[7]

Adjudication. Adjudication is the resolution of conflict between members of different groups in the society by political means. Because of the broad meaning we have given here to the word "political," this includes a wide range of actions, from an elder resolving a quarrel among his young kinsmen to peace-making between alien societies. We need not go so far as to include a father or mother settling a quarrel among their own children, but it must be clear that we are, nevertheless, dealing with personal, face-to-face sets of relationships. Thus what is of great concern is how do quarrels, feuds, even wars, end when there is no state, law court, or other formal means of adjudication? In other words, how is peace maintained in the absence of a public power standing over society and suppressing internal conflicts through legal means?

It has seemed to writers who lacked actual knowledge of primitive hunting-gathering societies that, inasmuch as the right to use force was not reserved to any governmental body, but was instead the private right of any person, society itself would be torn apart by a "war of every man against every man,"

---

[6] Elizabeth Marshall Thomas, *The Harmless People* (New York: Alfred A. Knopf, 1959), p. 183.

[7] June Helm MacNeish, "Leadership among the Northern Athabascans," *Anthropologica*, No. 2 (1956), 151.

as the philosopher Hobbes envisioned it. The fact of the matter, of course, is that band societies are not riven into pieces even though there are no formal adjudicative bodies to hold them together. But how are they held together in the face of this private right of every person and every kin group?

The right of persons to rectify their own wrongs has a legal name, *lex talionis*, the meaning of which is essentially given in the old Biblical expression, "an eye for an eye and a tooth for a tooth." There is in fact a tendency in primitive society to retaliate in precisely this way. On the face of it this would seem to mean that a state of perpetual feud and warfare must obtain.

The actual facts are rather surprising, however. Peace within the band is the normal condition, not the war of every man against every man. It is also rare that there is actual fighting among bands. Could it be that in the absence of police, law courts, and formal adjudicative bodies quarreling, feud, and warfare are so clearly and obviously dangerous that the people strive hard to avoid difficulties?

If for every damage there must be counter-damage, and for every insult a counter-insult, and if for every killing there must be another life taken, feud is likely, and feud by its nature tends to perpetuate itself. It is probable that everyone in a band society could remember a feud or have heard of one in the past. It is entirely possible, therefore, that everyone would know how disadvantageous a long drawn-out feud is. This must explain some of the things we often read of: how a band or even a family itself may punish one of its own members rather than have the aggrieved outsider take his counter-revenge. This would be simply because the danger of feud is appreciated by everyone.

But although feuds and warfare are relatively rare in band societies, they do consistently *threaten* and there must be some way of stopping them or of preventing their spread. Often they begin as mere quarrels between individuals, and for this reason it is important to stop them early. Within a given community the adjudication of a quarrel between two persons will ordinarily be handled by an elder who is a common relative of them both. It would be ideal if this person were in the same relationship to each one of the quarreling men, for then it would be evident that he would not be so likely to take sides. But of course this is not always the case, nor is it always possible that the person in this kinship status position might want to adjudicate. Sometimes one person is clearly enough in the right and the other in the wrong, or one person popular and the other unpopular, that the public becomes the adjudicator and the case is settled as soon as this common opinion becomes well-known.

When quarrels are not settled in any of the above ways, then some form of contest is held, preferably a game, that takes the place of an outright battle. Wrestling or head-butting contests are typical forms of quasi-dueling in Eskimo society. It is done in public and the winner is considered by the public to have won his case. But more common, and certainly more interesting, is the famous Eskimo song duel: the weapons used are words, "little, sharp words, like the wooden splinters which I hack off with my axe."

Song duels are used to work off grudges and disputes of all orders, save murder. An East Greenlander, however, may seek his satisfaction for the murder of a relative through a song contest if he is physically too weak to gain his end, or if he is so skilled in singing as to feel certain of victory. Inasmuch as East Greenlanders get so engrossed in the mere artistry of singing as to forget the cause of the grudge, this is understandable. Singing skill among these Eskimos equals or outranks gross physical prowess.

The singing style is highly conventionalized. The successful singer uses the traditional patterns of composition which he attempts to deliver with such finesse as to delight the audience to enthusiastic applause. He who is most heartily applauded is "winner." To win a song contest brings no restitution in its train. The sole advantage is in prestige.[8]

One of the advantages of the song duel carried on at length is that it gives the public time to come to a consensus about who is correct or who should admit guilt in the dispute. Ordinarily, people have some idea of whose side they are on, but as in most primitive communities the unanimity of the community as a whole is felt to be so desirable that it takes a while before the people can find out where the majority opinion lies. Gradually more people are laughing a little harder at one of the duelist's verses than at the other's, until it becomes apparent where the sympathy of the community lies, and then opinion quickly becomes unanimous and the loser retires in discomfiture.

Among Australian aborigines disputes are often settled through a ritualized spear-throwing duel. When a dispute is between an accuser and a defendant, which is commonly the case, the accuser ritually hurls the spears from a prescribed distance, while the defendant dodges them. The public can applaud the speed, force, and accuracy of the accuser as he hurls his spears, or they can applaud the adroitness with which the defendant dodges them. After a time unanimity is achieved as the approval for one or the other's skill gradually becomes overwhelming. When the defendant realizes that the community is finally considering him guilty, he is supposed to fail to dodge a spear and allow himself to be wounded in some fleshy part of his body. Conversely, the accuser simply stops throwing the spears when he becomes aware that public opinion is going against him.[9]

We have been discussing the ways disputes are settled between members of the same community. But much more dangerous and much more difficult to adjudicate are quarrels between people who are distantly related—that is, who are from different bands. The more distant the relationship or the more unknown the two groups are to each other, the more likely that an injury, when countered, will develop into a full-scale feud, simply because there are not enough people known to both groups who have the power to adjudicate

---

[8] E. A. Hoebel, *The Law of Primitive Man* (Cambridge: Harvard University Press, 1954), p. 93.

[9] C. W. M. Hart and Arnold R. Pilling, *The Tiwi of North Australia, Case Studies in Cultural Anthropology* (New York: Holt, Rinehart and Winston, 1960), 80–83.

the difficulties. A kinship community such as a band is solid in its external relations. Thus ordinarily the band as a whole undertakes to avenge an injury to one of its members. As a corollary of this, it is also usual, assuming that the other band is relatively distant, that the counter-injury to any of its members will serve. That is, the band as a whole is avenger and the other band is the culprit, so an injury to any member will serve the law.

Retribution, as in feud, is always recognized as a faulty jural mechanism because it does not ordinarily result in a return to the original state of balance. This is simply because the two contenders do not ordinarily view the injury in the same light, and it is unlikely that they will agree on what is equivalent retaliation to the original injury. But even so there are interesting attempts on the part of certain primitive peoples to prevent feud by means of what could be called "expiatory encounters." In the case of many aboriginal Australian societies, for example, when there has been a homicide, the guilty person has to submit himself to a shower of spears hurled at him by kinsmen of the slain person. Once he is wounded an end to the vendetta is possible, even though the retaliation was not in full. It is also common in

South African Bushman with dart. (Constance Stuart from Black Star.)

most primitive societies that the band of the culprit may punish him before the other band can retaliate—again, in order to prevent feuding.

There is an old Arab proverb that goes something like this: "I against my brother; I and my brother against my cousin; I, my brothers, and my cousins against the next village; all of us against the foreigner." Quarrels between close relatives, blood feuds between more distant relatives, warfare among those who are not related at all tends to involve solidarity rings or circles of relatives in primitive society just as the proverb would have it. In hunting-gathering societies there is no regulatory or adjudicative body or procedure to prevent warfare any more than there is to prevent feuds. It is something the public at large in informal ways must attempt to prevent. But in any case warfare is relatively rare and it is not usually bloody.

There are many reasons why warfare should not be expected to be intense, or prolonged among hunting-gathering bands of people, but the lack of strong organization must be an important factor. War is a dangerous business and to run the risk of death is contrary to basic biological tendencies. In the absence of an organization that can mobilize or draft warriors, direct them, and give them reasons to fight, one does not expect that much real fighting will occur. Compelling modern reasons, such as the strong ethical and religious sanctions by a strong state controlling mass communication, and the authority that can command obedience by physical punishment, by threat of death for desertion, and so on, are missing in primitive societies. Another matter related to organization is logistics. A hunting and gathering economy simply cannot sustain a military effort for a protracted period because of the lack of stored food.

Perhaps most important of all is the fact that at the hunting-gathering level of development there is no important economic stimulus to full-scale war. The birth-death ratio in hunting-gathering societies is such that it would be rare for population pressure to cause some part of the population to fight others for territorial acquisition. Even if such a circumstance occurred it would not lead to much of a battle. The stronger, more numerous, group would simply prevail, probably even without a battle, if hunting rights or rights to some gathering spot were demanded. In the second place there is not much to gain by plunder in hunting-gathering society. All bands are poor in material goods and there are no standard items of exchange that serve as capital or as valuables. Finally, at the hunting-gathering level the acquisition of captives to serve as slaves for economic exploitation—a common cause of warfare in more modern times—would be useless, given the low productivity of the economy. Captives and slaves would have a difficult time producing more than enough food to sustain themselves.

At any rate, warfare is exceptional at the band level of society and it is not prolonged nor is the death toll great. Usually the occasion for any kind of battle or threat of battle is some kind of personal conflict, often caused by an elopement, or an illegal love affair of some kind, or simply an insult. There seems to be no evidence whatsoever in any of the band societies under review that warfare is actually undertaken for economic reasons, such as for booty or territorial acquisition. But the dangers and fears are there and this is an important political factor in any band society.

Five *Ideology*

In a sense, ideology is the most distinctively human of the conventional divisions of culture, for if culture issues from a mental ability peculiar to man among all animals, and since ideology is that aspect of culture most purely mental, then it is the most basic and direct indicator of our humanness. That it is conventionally treated last—as a "superstructure"—should not suggest a relative insignificance. From a long range, evolutionary point of view we see that important aspects of ideology are limited by, in some respects determined by, characteristics of the technology, economy, social system, and even the habitat. It is therefore easier to discuss ideology on a comparative basis after these various impingements have been covered. But this does not mean that the action is one-sided. In a general sense, the other aspects of culture depend on the human ability to think and communicate symbolically in the first place.

What is ideology? What are we discussing? Simply this. We want to talk about the intellectual patterns characteristic of a type of society. To put it another way, ideology connotes a society's conceptions, its beliefs, about things. Not an individual's sometimes idiosyncratic ideas, but the forms of knowledge that a culture imparts *to* the individuals in the society are what we want to talk about.

But this "knowledge" includes an enormous range of kinds of ideas. It includes ideas about the hereafter, about the chemical properties of things, about counting things and reckoning time, about etiquette, pleasure, medicine, proper attitudes, how to perform a ritual, how to kill people, play music, bury the dead, and decorate a nubile female. Evidently we should divide ideology into more manageable aspects, particularly because we should want to relate ideological matters to a functional context. What does ideology do? Lots of things, obviously. A religious ritual can relieve psychic stress; a code of etiquette smooths social relations; an art form pleases the gods; a mathematical formula can result in a new man-made chemical compound; and so on.

An important function of much of ideology is simply explication. In anthropology it is fairly conventional to distinguish two kinds of explanatory statements, the *existential* and the *normative*. Existential explanations are concerned with what is thought to be actually "out there" and how to deal with it. This is usually a utilitarian context and often has to do with physical objects. But sometimes, of course, the knowledge is of no use (except to satisfy, perhaps, an urge to know or to seem to know), or it may be completely false, or may refer to something that does not exist. Even a purposely false statement made to a child ("Santa Claus is coming tonight") is every bit as existential a statement as one which says that water is composed of H_2O. One is false, the other true, but the purpose of both statements is to impart some kind of information about the external world.

There is another way to put it. Existential statements include all statements about things and their properties that are not normative. Normative statements explain things or events in terms of such qualities as good or bad, what ought to be, what is desirable. This category of ideas functions most usually in the context of social relations, having to do with proper behavior, codes of etiquette, ethics, morals, and the like.

It is useful to divide ideology into these two aspects because, although all societies have both, they may coexist in very different proportions and relative elaboration. The contrast between primitive bands and modern civilization in this, as in other matters, is particularly striking. In very primitive societies, normative ideology bulks large and the existential is very limited; and, of course, the existential ideology in modern society is not only enormously large and complex but part of it is even institutionalized separately as science.

In order again to make explicit the contrast of primitive and modern society, it is useful to name another broad distinction between kinds of ideas: *naturalistic* and *supernaturalistic*. Naturalistic ideas are those that refer, or purport to refer, to things and events in nature, as nature reveals itself to the senses. Supernaturalistic ideas are only "made up" verbally, so to speak, and do not refer to the sensed properties of nature. Man is forever restricted in his naturalistic knowledge, and primitive man is particularly restricted because of a rudimentary technology. But with respect to supernaturalism, not even "the sky's the limit." Here again the contrast is enormous between primitive and modern society. The expression and organization of naturalistic knowledge is minute and simple in primitive society; and supernaturalism, proportionately great. But it seems that as naturalistic knowledge grows during the evolution of culture it diminishes supernaturalism, encroaches on its territory, so that in modern society many people may go to church an hour a week but otherwise give very little heed to supernaturalism.

Somehow related, but somehow different from what has been discussed so far, are such things as painting, music, ritual, poetry, and myth. They all "say" something, convey information (even if only feelings), and any of these is sometimes supernaturalistic or naturalistic, existential in intent or normative (or perhaps not clearly any single one of these). It would seem that these kinds of things differ from the other categories of ideology in their mode of expression and perpetuation. That is, any bit of information, be it naturalistic or supernaturalistic, existential or normative, can be expressed in either of two ways, in *artistic* form or in *mundane* form. The essence of art is that the idea, feeling, or emotion is expressed indirectly. The mundane expression of an idea, on the other hand, is straightforward. The most straightforward and thus the least artful expressions are, of course, mathematical formulas. Most everyday verbal statements are much more clumsy, redundant, inaccurate, and ambiguous, but that is the fault of the language. The expression is mundane unless an intentional indirectness is introduced. There are, of course, differences in the amount and kind of indirection in various art forms. Myths, poetry, and drama introduce only some indirection; rituals, sculpture, and painting more; the dance still more; and probably music the most.

One of the trends in the evolution of culture is the elaboration of both mundane and artistic expression due to technical improvements and the rise of specialists. Equally noticeable is the rise of more kinds of expression. This is especially apparent with respect to art forms. But it is noteworthy that any *particular* art form that may exist in a primitive society—ivory figurines among the Eskimo, Paleolithic cave drawings, the paintings of the Arunta—may be favorably compared with that kind of art form in modern society. Indirection is indirection, and it can be done "just right" sometimes, at any level of cultural development.

Existential Ideology
in Band Society

Existential ideas can be either naturalistic or supernaturalistic. We have just stated that supernaturalism occupies a larger ideological space, and naturalism much less, in primitive society than in modern society. Let us not underplay the significance or the amount of actual naturalistic knowledge an *individual* might have, however, in a hunting-gathering society. Such people are closer to nature, more directly dependent on it, than people in higher societies. It would be surprising if they did not possess a great deal of factual information about the habits of the animals and plants they live on, as well as the properties of the inorganic environment.

But what individuals might know is not truly a part of the society's ideology until it assumes a more abstract expression so that it can be imparted to others. The naturalistic knowledge of primitive peoples is largely linked to the individual's articulation with nature; it is not like a science or a philosophy of natural*ism*. The Eskimo igloo is a marvelous contrivance for containing and circulating heated air, and the Eskimo build it with seemingly exact knowledge of how warmed air behaves. But Vilhjalmur Stefansson relates that, try as he would, he could not get his Eskimo friends to recognize the abstract generalization that heat rises. All they could say is that this is the right way to build an igloo. Neither this, nor the knowledge of the habits of plants and animals, is a subject for debate, or of classroom-like instruction. One learns these things largely by imitation, and ordinarily in the context in which the knowledge is used—hunting techniques are learned by going hunting with more experienced companions.

Furthermore, even the amount of purely pragmatic information is bound to be limited simply because of the rudimentary technology of hunting-gathering societies. Another aspect of this is a lack of specialization; nobody is at work discovering things to be imparted at large for the good of the society. Perhaps this lack of specialization is the reason for the lack of abstraction and generalization, as well as the absence of philosophizing about nature. It has often been asked, do primitive peoples understand cause-and-effect? In one sense they do, of course, as must anyone who has a normal contingent relationship to nature. But in an important sense primitive peoples do not seem to know the *principle* of cause-and-effect; it is not formulated as an abstraction. This is much like saying that although primitive persons must have some sense, for example, of geometrical relations, they do not have a geometry as such. Similarly, it appears that they know nothing of mathematics, although they can count in a rudimentary way.

Anaxagoras said that man is the wisest of animals because he has hands. It would seem that one exemplification of this is that, in origin, systems of numeration were determined by the fact that humans have five fingers on each hand; for fives and tens, or fives and twenties, seem to be the basis for nearly all counting systems. Most hunting-gathering societies numerate to four or five only. After that comes "many" and "very many." It is interesting that there is an even simpler number system, the binary, but it has come about late in modern times to be used on digital computers. The binary system proceeds from just two entities, making more elaborate combinations by a simple additive process. There are a few groups of Australian aborigines whose method of reckoning is also binary, as follows:

Urupum	(1)
Okosa	(2)
Okosa-Urupun	(3)
Okosa-Okosa	(4)
Okosa-Okosa-Urupun	(5)
Okosa-Okosa-Okosa	(6)

Whereas the above is the additive process that is the essence of modern binary arithmetic, there is a difference which is essentially the difference between primitiveness in numeration and sophistication. These aborigines do not reckon *beyond* six; everything from seven to seven million is just "many" or "very many." But let it be emphasized that this is due to the simplicity of the society and not to the simplicity of the people's brains. There are few things to count, in the first place, and of course the economy is not based on accounting, and the technology needs no mathematics.

As with space and number, so it is with time. In simple band societies there is no need to measure time in detailed units; a day, the lunar cycle, a generation will usually suffice for most purposes. Activities are sporadic rather than repetitive. Thus passage of time is surely recognized, but the ideology is not required to make explicit a great number of temporal units.

Related to conceptions of time, of course, are conceptions of history and evolution. Primitive societies seem essentially ahistorical and nonevolutionary in their beliefs about themselves as a society. They, their culture, their habitat, once created (usually by some spiritual culture-hero) have simply maintained equilibrium. Nothing has been altered since the creation and no future change is expected. Customs do not grow and change, nor do they have "reasons" or causes, for these, of course, would be discoverable only through an investigation of their actual origin and growth. Expectably, then, primitive peoples are not inclined to criticize or challenge their culture, much less to attempt to change it. It would seem that an ideology that includes conceptions of historical fortune and of development must come out of a culture that has in fact gone through such changes, as has Euro-American civilization.

To the extent that naturalism is restricted as a philosophy, so supernaturalism is expanded. There is nothing in heaven or on earth that cannot be explained by supernatural means. That concomitant of ignorance, omniscience, is one of the striking characteristics of primitive peoples. The less a people knows, in the naturalistic sense, the more it seems to know, and can think it knows, by employing supernaturalism. And the concomitant of knowledge, control, follows the same route. Little attempt is made to control nature by naturalistic means, but a great deal of social time goes into the attempt at control by supernatural means. A sacrifice propitiates the spirit who withholds rain; another spirit, summoned by the shaman, diagnoses an illness; amulets, always carried, guard against misfortunes. Every "thing" in nature has a spirit which not only is the explanation of its characteristics, but also provides a means for human beings to influence it.

These spirits are not gods. Even the apparently important culture-heroes or creator spirits who gave the people life, stocked the rivers and forests, taught the arts, and so on, are not much more than explanatory devices. They no longer intervene in human affairs, hence they are not worshiped, propitiated, or scolded. They do not watch over the people, and they do not exert a moral force. Their function is with respect to existential ideology rather than the normative.

Those spirits that are present (rather than belonging to the misty past of the creator spirits) are individual spirits, with distinctive attributes or personalities. This is related to the fact that individual persons in the society are those who contact the spirit. With the exception of the curing shaman, who usually has a special spirit who diagnoses illnesses for him, there is no restriction on contacting the supernatural, very little public worship, no temples, and no mediation by a priesthood.

In heaven as it is on earth; humans can only project from what they know. A band society is a highly personal society, and the spirit world is thus highly individualized. A band society is also egalitarian and the spirit world reflects this by a corresponding lack of hierarchy among the spirits. But a band society also has groups within it, so that sometimes we find what E. B. Tylor called species spirits (these are more usually regarded as totemic spirits). A particular group may consider itself related to, perhaps descended from, some particular plant or animal species. The relationship is manifested ritually, ordinarily with the avowed purpose of promoting the welfare and numbers of the species for the good of other groups in the society. The Australian natives have elaborated this social ideology more than most other hunters and gatherers.

Human beings, of course, also are believed to have spirits or souls. Death is due to the departure of the soul; illness, especially where it is accompanied by unconsciousness or illusions, is usually thought of as due to the temporary absence of the soul; dreams, apparently universally among primitives, are the adventuring abroad of the soul; ghosts, of course, are the liberated souls of the dead. The idea of the soul, above all, is related to the comforting belief in the afterlife.

The characteristics that human souls are believed to have are closely related to the matter of control, particularly as this control or influence operates in regard to the most poignant and socially disturbing aspects of the human condition—illness and death. The most striking as well as the most nearly universal form of control in primitive society is called *shamanism*.

Any person may, by appropriate means, establish contact with the spirit world. But some people are able to convince the rest of the society that they excel at it. And of course when illness threatens a person the relatives want the best help available, hence the tendency for some one person to become more specialized than the rest, even though originally he was believed to be only slightly superior in his ability to contact the spirit world. This shaman (the Tungusic word for medicine-man) is not a professional specialist but rather a leisure-time specialist; he cannot "do well by doing good," for the society's economy cannot support full-time specialists—the shaman hunts and fishes like the rest of the men. A shaman is thus a religious practitioner of sorts, but not part of a true priesthood.

The typical form of shamanistic contact with the spirits is by *possession*. At the ritualized performance, the spirit enters the shaman and uses his body and voice as a medium of expression ("the spirit moves him"). Usually the performance features dancing, chanting, or tambourine drumming, sometimes to exceedingly monotonous lengths (especially among the Eskimo), until the audience as well as the shaman is in a highly suggestible mood. Sometimes the unconsciousness of the shaman permits his own spirit to liberate itself from his body and journey in the spirit world to find out who caused the illness.

Shamanism is usually, though not always, restricted to men. It does not require formal training (another difference from true priesthood), although some of the tricks of the trade may be passed on from father to son. But a shamanistic bent does seem to require a kind of psychic ebullience that enables a person to go into trance or have hysteria or hallucinations. Sometimes the shamans described in primitive societies are physiologically or psychologically sick, and would be undergoing treatment in our own society. Epileptics, for example, are viewed with awe in most primitive societies and are often shamans, because the seizures seem like spirit possession.

The standard job of the shaman is to diagnose and cure illness. Illness is supernaturally caused and supernaturally explained—the most common causes are soul loss (or theft of the soul), possession by evil spirits who are taking vengeance or who have been "sent" by sorcerers, and the intrusion of foreign objects into the sick person's body by sorcery. Thus the diagnosis is simply to divine the "who" that did it or the "what" (*e.g.*, the foreign object) that was done to the victim. Once the cause is diagnosed, counter-magic against the sorcerer or mere removal of the foreign object by magic (or the shaman's sleight-of-hand, usually) is all that is required to put the patient on his feet again.

Does this treatment ever really work? The answer, if modern psychology is in some degree correct, must be that sometimes it does, or does somewhat. Many illnesses are purely psychosomatic, and others that are not are frequently responsive to the psychological state of the ill person. The belief in sorcery is so firm that we have in ethnographic writings many instances of apparent cure of true illness, and, more striking, cases of illness and even death caused by the person's belief that he had been bewitched. But of course not all attempts at sorcery result in the victim's death, nor do all shamans' attempts at saving people succeed. But this need not result in any loss of faith in witchcraft or shamanism because the blame is easily shifted in the complex spirit world—a more powerful spirit intervenes and circumvents the attempts of the shaman or sorcerer.

Shamans are essentially concerned with illness, but occasionally their superior divinitory powers are employed in other ways. They may be asked to forecast the weather, find lost objects, predict the coming of game, and so on. But in none of these cases is the shaman a religious functionary in the way a true priest is. In fact, when the band, or some such group, performs religious ceremonials that have social significance—as in the Australian totemic rites—then the presiding leaders are not shamans but elders who occupy this post because they are respected for their age and because they know more about the rites. But these leaders do not mediate between the people and the spirit world as true religious functionaries do; they merely regulate the rituals. In a literal sense, these old men are simply the "masters of ceremony."

Normative Ideology
in Band Societies

A society's rules of social conduct and of morality, like existential knowledge, can be placed in either a naturalistic or supernaturalistic context. In our own society we are accustomed to having morality "preached" in church, in a supernatural context. Etiquette, on the other hand, is entirely different from morality, perhaps because it is taught more exclusively within the family rather than in a public religious congregation. But this makes a misleading, ethnocentric point of departure for a discussion of normative beliefs in primitive society. In the first place, primitive religious ideology has no moral or ethical content whatsoever. In the second place, because band societies are small and based on kinship, morality is taught within the family, just as is etiquette. As a matter of fact, it is difficult to separate etiquette from morality in family-band societies, and is perhaps fruitless to try. Let us, instead, begin the easier way, by talking about normative rules in general, as comprising ethics, morality, etiquette, any rules about conduct that are made for the good of the society.

Normative ideology is a society's cultural device for transforming, sublimating, or otherwise constraining individual propensities and desires into forms of behavior that serve wider social ends. It exists because of the innumerable ways in which an individual's desires are in conflict with his society. The normative ideology is not entirely made up of simple rules, of course, which if broken are straightforwardly punished, like a breach of law. Often the "rules" are implicit only, and the person who breaches them is punished, if at all, only by a slight loss of prestige—he is "not a kind person" or is "not thoughtful of others." And many of the normative values may be so covertly punished in the breach that nobody, literally, knows of it. This is a way of referring to that quintessentially human characteristic, conscience. Conscience, when it wins a battle all by itself, is a sign of the victory of society over its worst enemy, the individual with his or her insatiable ego.

Normative rules, attitudes, and values—overt and covert—vary from society to society depending on the problems posed by the nature of the social order. In primitive hunting-gathering societies, the social order is based on kinship, however broadly conceived, and the problems of internal order are those of a personal, face-to-face nature rather than the familiar political ones of our own society. The normative ideology of bands, therefore, is familistic, and the closest analogies to it from modern society are to be found in the values and rules of family life.

Most of the values we "hold dear" are the familistic ones. Love, generosity, mutual aid, cooperation, are all appropriate, in some measure necessary, to the functioning of small face-to-face groups like households. When these are preached, however, as morality in our society, then we are being admonished to extend these wholesome sentiments into the larger society. And they must be constantly preached and "pushed," for it is not at all clear that love and generosity are always appropriate attitudes to take in the market economy, the political power struggle, or international relations, or for that matter even most sports and recreations ("Nice guys finish last").

These sentiments and values are not preached nor buttressed by threat of religious reprisal in band societies because they do not need to be. There is no larger, impersonal context of behavior where it is difficult to practice them. Thus the rules that create respectful distance in behavior toward a mother- or father-in-law also function to preserve some love, mitigate jealousy, create reciprocity, and so on. They do not say, "love your mother's brother," or "be generous to your father-in-law" so much as to describe the forms of behavior that are required. Thus the patterned form of address to the mother's brother is what is taught, and the appropriate kind of gift and when to give it and how to give it is the *form* that generosity takes. Thus etiquette seems so important; it is the formal aspect of a kind of morality. But by its nature—because it is formal—it is explicit, whereas the familistic morality behind it is more often vague and implicit. Clearly "love," for instance, can be strongly present in a social order without people making rules about it. In fact, the necessity in our society for explicit moral preachings and teachings about such things as love and honesty is probably good evidence that we are worried about the frequency of hate and dishonesty. But we must remember that we worry mostly about morality in the larger society, outside the sphere of kindred and close friends. Primitive people do not have these worries because they do not conceive of—do not *have*—the larger society to adjust to. The ethic does not extend to strangers; they are simply enemies, not even "people."

Artistic Expression
in Band Societies

Technology, the character and complexity of society, the general nature of the ideology, all have something to do with the way artistic development proceeds. Primitive bands lie at the evolutionary extreme from modern civilization in all these respects and we may expect, therefore, that in some general way the art will be commensurately at a remove from our own.

The simple technology and absence of specialization in hunting-gathering societies obviously prevent the development of many artistic techniques. Forms of literary art are completely absent, of course, and instrumental music is restricted to rude rhythm-beaters of one kind or another. Except for the sporadic use of simple design painting and sculpture, artistic expression is largely confined to the forms that do not require tools or "props." These forms are predominantly oral tradition, particularly mythology, accompanied by song, dance, and ritual drama.

The lack of complexity in the society means that artistic expression is not confined to a few specialists, nor is it esoteric in intent. It is "people's art" because everyone can appreciate it, and even participate in much of it, and it means the same thing to all.

The ideology in general, it may be repeated, stands in strong contrast to that of modern civilization with respect to the emphasis on supernaturalism over naturalism. It would follow, therefore, that the most usual context for artistic expression in hunting-gathering society is the supernatural. Thus the most usual art forms in band societies—myth, ritual and ceremony, song and dance, even the less prevalent graphic arts—are also most usually performed religiously and in close association to one another.

Mythology has striking general similarities throughout the range of band societies. Apparently universally there are standardized origin myths and tales of the heroes who created the people, gave them their customs, kindled fire, taught the arts, molded the landscape, stocked it with game, and so on. The following Andamanese version of their origin is fairly typical:

> The first man was *Jutpu*. He was born inside the joint of a big bamboo, just like a bird in an egg. The bamboo split and he came out. He was a little child. When it rained he made a small hut for himself and lived in it. He made little bows and arrows. As he grew bigger he made bigger huts, and bigger bows and arrows. One day he found a lump of quartz and with it he scarified himself. *Jutpu* was lonely, living all by himself. He took some clay (kọt) from a nest of the white ants and moulded it into the shape of woman. She became alive and became his wife. She was called *Kọt*. They lived together at *Teraut-buliu*. Afterwards *Jutpu* made other people out of clay. These were the ancestors. *Jutpu* taught them how to make canoes and bows and arrows, and how to hunt and fish. His wife taught the women how to make baskets and nets and mats and belts, and how to use clay for making patterns on the body.[1]

Many myths are closely associated with ritual, and often with singing and dancing. A common interpretation of this association has been that these latter are appurtenances of the myths, added dimensions to the communication of the stories, imparting emotions and meanings that words alone cannot accomplish. If one thinks of ritual as a sort of dramatization of the mythical story-line, even in a very loose sense, then it would seem that ritual is subsequent to and dependent on myth. And further, it suggests that the very origin of art is related to the supernaturalism of existential belief.

Such assumptions have been challenged, however, by A. R. Radcliffe-Brown, and his argument is convincing.[2] There is good reason for viewing ritual and ceremony as both prior to and more persistent than myth, that it is ritual or ceremony that symbolizes social feelings and sentiments and that "do" something to the spirit world as well as to the society of participants —myth thus appearing as a *post hoc* rationalization. Confucius said it:

> The ancient kings were watchful in regard to the things by which the mind was affected. And so they instituted ceremonies to direct men's

---

[1] A. R. Radcliffe-Brown, *The Andaman Islanders* (Glencoe: The Free Press, 1948), p. 192.

[2] A. R. Radcliffe-Brown, "Religion and Society," *Structure and Function in Primitive Society* (Glencoe: The Free Press, 1952), pp. 158–177.

aims aright; music to give harmony to their voices; laws to unify their conduct; and punishments to guard against their tendencies to evil. The end to which ceremonies, music, punishments and laws conduct is one; they are the instruments by which the minds of the people are assimilated, and good order in government is made to appear.[3]

One of the striking things about ritual is its persistence in the face of different interpretations of its meaning. As an example, consider the variations in the Roman, Greek Orthodox, and Anglican explanations of the same baptismal and communion rites. Or consider burial and mourning rites and their persistence in modern times among people whose ideas vary from complete faith in a happy afterlife to those of atheism.

Ritual clearly does something; it has social consequences that myth does not have. Rituals submerge individuals in groups, improve an *esprit de corps*, are "instruments of good order." "The family that prays together stays together." There are peoples and nations that disavow religion, oppose churches, or profess a philosophy rather than a mythology, but there are no societies that lack ritual and ceremony.

If ritual and ceremony have important social functions, then the nature of the society will have some general influence on the nature of the rituals. As we have mentioned so often, the nature of hunting-gathering societies is preeminently personal and familistic. This would mean, of course, that the rituals and ceremonies would have to do with the exigencies of family life, and obviously would not be used by national governments, state-churches, courtiers, and the like.

All families in the world, in whatever society, have rituals of some sort connected with birth, marriage, and death. Many, but not all, also have rituals connected with the change from childhood to adolescent status. These four ritual occasions are called by anthropologists *Life Crisis Rites*, or in French, *Rites de Passage*. Hunting-gathering societies celebrate these occasions, of course, but because there are ordinarily no others so important in a familistic society they are more visibly characteristic of bands.

Of the various life crisis rites, those involving the initiation of adolescents, or puberty rites, are the most distinctive at the band level. Birth, marriage, and burial rituals are individualized, occur sporadically, and in the case of birth and death, at least, they happen when they happen. The physiological onset of adulthood, on the other hand, is gradual, and a year or two of difference is not significant, so that it is possible to have one big celebration for children of somewhat different ages from several families. Thus the rites of initiation to adulthood seem more socially significant and larger in scale than the others. To put it another way, the initiation rites seem to be of group interest, whereas birth, marriage, and death are of more concern to the immediate family, less so for the more distant relatives.

The more spectacular and elaborate ceremonies involve the initiation of boys. Almost universal features of these ceremonies are physical ordeals, such

---

[3] Quoted by Radcliffe-Brown, *op. cit.*, pp. 158–159.

as scarification, and the ritual taking of the boys from the company of women and children for imparting to them secret religious lore which is known to initiated men only. The Ona and Yahgan of Tierra del Fuego stage a dramatic myth, the theme of which is that once women dominated society until the males were finally able to band together secretly and with ritual sources of power finally defeat them. Such a Thurberesque theme points up sharply one of the most significant changes when a boy suddenly becomes a man and joins men's society, the completely altered nature of his subsequent relationship to women.

As in so many aspects of ritual, ceremony, and myth the Australian natives have elaborated initiation ceremonies beyond those found in most of the primitive world. The following description, though condensed, should give some sense of the richness and significance of the occasion.[4]

Initiation of Boys in Australia

The Taking of the Novice.   There is a prescribed, highly ritualized manner by which the novice is taken from his family to join the other boys who will undergo initiation. The women cry and try (or pretend to try) to forcibly keep the boy. The elders who have removed him from his family then paint his body in ritual designs, toss him in the air, bite his scalp till blood flows, and finally pierce his nasal septum.

Ceremonial Welcome.   As the various groups of elders come with their novices to the ceremonial place they welcome one another and fix their sleeping places in a prescribed arrangement, facing their home camp. A ritualized combat is a frequent feature of the welcome, after which, with old grievances thus settled, a great feast is prepared.

Death Ceremony.   The individual novices next undergo a ceremony which resembles the death ritual, apparently to symbolize the death of the child (to be reborn later as an adult). Usually the novices are carried as though lifeless while the female relatives chant dirges, weeping copiously.

The Ritual Operations.   Circumcision is the usual operation, and it signalizes the beginning of the period of seclusion and initiation into ritual secrets. Among many groups cicatrices are cut in the boy and an incisor tooth is knocked out.

---

[4] Paraphrased from A. P. Elkin, *The Australian Aborigines* (New York: Doubleday & Company, Inc., 1954), pp. 171–179. Used by permission.

The Seclusion. The foregoing operations have "killed" the novices, who are now kept in a secret place, each tended by a special instructor. They are gradually taught more of the customs of the society and introduced to sacred places. This period may last up to a year in some parts of Australia.

The Blood Ceremony. This is a very important ceremony, for it unites the initiates with the elders and consequently with the earlier ancestors. Blood is drawn from the arms of the elders and the novices are anointed with it, and in some areas they drink it. The elders also anoint themselves with (or drink) one another's blood. Special songs ritualize these acts, which consecrate them, so to speak, as a form of sacrament.

The Fire Ceremony. This is an ordeal-type of ritual during which the candidates are passed through smoke, coals are dropped on them, and they may have to trample on coals and ashes.

The Washing. A ceremonial washing is supposed to clean off all traces of the sacred world to which the boys have been exposed. This purification must occur before the return to normal life; that is, before having any contact with the uninitiated women and children. On their return home, the newly-initiated youths are welcomed as though returned from the dead.

Music and dance are closely associated with religious ceremonies in all band societies. The graphic arts, which seem more purely art to us, are also religious in function (and perhaps in origin). Art-making, apparently of any kind, is an aspect of primitive man's attempt to control nature and society by supernatural means, and it is as ritualized as any of the other supernatural means.[5] This is, of course, in strong contrast to what modern people usually think of art and of the role of the artist. But there is no "art for art's sake" in primitive societies, nor art that exists solely to satisfy an individual's feelings and emotions—whether of the artist himself or of the beholder. This is not to say that there are no personal satisfactions at all in primitive art-making, for presumably there are, but only that art has not become detached from its religious function to become a self-sufficient, specialized and institutionalized end in itself.

We see here, as so often in other contexts, the essential contrast between our own highly specialized society and one which does not have clearly differentiated and institutionalized aspects of culture and behavior. Just as it is difficult to say just what artifacts, groups, and actions are economic, or political, or religious in primitive societies, so it is difficult to judge what is

---

[5] See the interesting discussion of the ritual nature of art in Morton H. Levine, "Prehistoric Art and Ideology," *American Anthropologist*, Vol. 59 (1957), 949–962.

art and what is not. The usual definitions of art given in our society simply do not fit the case.

This is why it was necessary to define art as a kind of communication. But unlike mundane communication, it is indirect. Another way of suggesting its quality is to cite the element of mystery. Indirection lends mystery and mystery lends emotion. But it is only in this very broad sense that art is one of the universals of human culture. The functional context of art in band societies is religious ritual; the forms of art are limited in kind, and the aim is control (rather than to give "aesthetic pleasure"). Nor is the artist "creative." Quite the other way around, the style or pattern must be followed exactly simply because it is ritualized—any deviation breaks the spell just as surely as it does in an act of magic or sorcery.

Six Summary

In the preceding pages we have made some general observations about the nature of hunting-gathering societies and have cited a variety of illustrative materials. We also have taken pains to point out the most important contrasts between hunting-gathering societies and the cultures of modern nations. It is a way of trying to answer the question we asked in the beginning of the book: What is gained and what is lost when people acquire civilization? Inasmuch as the gains—especially the recent ones—are so obvious and so frequently extolled, it is appropriate now to direct attention to our possible losses.

The characteristics of hunting-gathering societies that are most different from those of modern societies lie mainly in those institutions that are related to the vast difference in the scale of the two kinds of societies. In fact, in the later stages of society which culminate in modern civilization, complex and formal organizations and institutions have appeared that have no counterpart whatsoever in primitive societies. The greatest similarities relate to comparisons between units of the societies that are comparable in scale

71

—most notably, domestic families—and of modes of behavior and artifacts related to them.

Sociologists, historians, political scientists, even anthropologists, are accustomed to analyzing culture into various parts and aspects. Usually the most prominent parts are assumed to be subsystems, such as the economic, social, political, and ideological. And then there is, of course, the modern functionalist view that these subsystems are not autonomous but dependent on each other. Thus the economic subsystem, so basic to the society because it supplies the material needs of the people, nevertheless demands social order and political support and in return is justified by the ideological subsystem. But one also considers the degrees of institutional autonomy and the ways in which a subsystem can be described and "understood" in formal terms—that is, in terms of the internal arrangement of its own parts.

The choice of chapter headings implies that something like the above form of analysis has been used here. But primitive society generally, and the very primitive societies like hunting-gathering bands especially, are so different from modern nations in scale and related complexity that it would seem necessary that any analytical scheme appropriate to modern society would have to be considerably modified before it could be used also for hunting-gathering societies. It is true that anthropologists have sometimes unintentionally distorted the nature of primitive culture by using, without sufficient modification and explanation, some of the analytical concepts from the social sciences that pertain to modern society.

Taking technology and economy as an example, we find first of all that among hunter-gatherers there are no separate organizations of people who perform technological tasks or engage in economic exchange. The organization is merely that of kinsmen. If at one time this group does technological or economic things, at another time the same organization may be performing political, ceremonial, or purely social tasks. Evidently we must think of technological and economic *contexts* of behavior, rather than economic organizations or institutions.

A number of other modern characteristics are missing from the economy of hunting-gathering peoples. There are no specialists who earn their livings at some particular economic task. In fact, there are no intermediaries of any kind; the technological and economic system is direct, from producer to consumer (when these are not in fact the same individual). The only division of labor is of sex and age distinctions of the sort found in any family. There are some tasks appropriate for the aged, others for grown adults, others for children of various ages, and, of course, male and female specialties.

Hunting-gathering band societies are not divided into classes of rich or poor families. In fact, there is no private property of the kind that would permit this kind of distinction. People do, however, pridefully own those kinds of items that have here been called *personalty*, items made and used by individuals—things like weapons, decorations, clothing, private rituals, amulets, and so on. Furthermore, the exchange of goods is conducted entirely in terms of reciprocity, never commercially. This reciprocity varies from the very general to the more specific forms depending on the social relations of those who exchange. The emotions as well as the etiquette of kinship, and the morality of modesty and generosity, all together dominate the exchange, rendering it a social act as well as an economic act.

Social obligations, in fact, so dominate the character of exchanges that in the usual modern meaning of the word there is no *economy* at all in band societies. Only if we use the broadest meaning of the word "economy" —the material, life-sustaining, provisioning activities of the society—can we properly speak of economy in hunting-gathering societies. Familistic kinds of reciprocities exist in all societies, and our own society therefore has some modest counterparts of, or analogies to, the form of economy in primitive society, but the broader impersonal system of market-style exchange of modern society is completely absent among bands.

As in the realm of economics, so in political organization. The hunting-gathering societies lack the formal legal and governmental structures that we are accustomed to in modern society. They have the same problems of decision-making with respect to concerted action and of adjudicating quarrels between persons and groups but have no formal institutions with which to solve them. There are problems of governance, but no governmental organization. There are also the same problems of controlling deviant behavior as there are in any society, but there are no formal laws and formal punishments, only customary norms and sanctions. Without a state, without government, without jails and police, without legal systems, how is authority wielded, then, in order to maintain the integrity of the society?

It might be imagined that in the absence of formal governmental and legal institutions a "strong man" would be necessary in order to personally punish deviants, lead the groups, and adjudicate in terms of his own personal authority. But surprisingly, band societies are characterized by a lack of authoritarian chiefs. In fact, so egalitarian is this kind of society and so restricted are the powers of any particular persons that it would seem better to speak of persons of *influence,* rather than persons of authority. One reason for preferring to use the term "influence" is because authority usually has to do with the exercise of power—the imposition of a person's will on others. In all state societies this is clearly a matter of force, and it is spelled out explicitly in terms of the law and the punishments that will be forthcoming in cases of breaches of the law. But band societies reject the authority of personal force, except of course the authority of a father over his children. An "influential person" in a band society connotes someone who has admirable qualities, such as wisdom and charity, rather than physical power. Superior physical force does not work; in band societies as in a group of schoolboys the overgrown bully gets his comeuppance sooner or later, often from a coalition of weaklings.

Influence is wielded in such informal ways that it is difficult to know always just how to characterize its action or its origin. One characteristic of an influential man would be simply his *charisma,* the influence he can exert by virtue of personal qualities that are admired by the people. The other factor is structural, by which a person of male sex and of appropriately advanced age is by virtue of that formal social status more likely to be in a position of political influence than are women or younger persons. But this, it should be emphasized, is an aspect of the kinship organization, not political organization. All we can say is that the social organization is that of kinship which operates sometimes in a context that we can consider economic, sometimes in a context that we can consider political. The same can be said for religion, art, or other ideological matters.

As we pointed out in the last chapter, ideology in band societies is pervasively supernaturalistic. To say this is not to belittle the great amount of naturalistic existential knowledge that primitive people must possess as individuals. Simply because they confront nature so directly they must know a lot about it. But the expression of existential knowledge, particularly in the context of explanation, remains anthropomorphic and supernaturalistic. As with explanation, so with the related matter of control. A great deal of social time goes into the attempt to control or influence nature by supernatural means. All things in nature have a spirit of some sort which is not only the way in which the actions or characteristics of the object are to be explained, but also the means by which the human beings influence or control them.

The normative ideology, the sentiments and values of the society, on the other hand, is not taught in the context of supernaturalism the way it is so often in our society. We receive many "preachings" of moral and ethical virtues, usually in church. In primitive societies these are more likely to be taught in formalistic ways rather than as abstract virtues. The ideal *forms* of behavior—proper demeanor—determines that moral or ethical behavior will be taken. Etiquette therefore looms importantly, as the formal aspect of the morality, whereas ethics as such, in the abstract, gets little expression.

Thus primitive behavior seems characterized by a great deal of supernaturalism with respect to the ideas about the world and by formalism with respect to valued kinds of conduct. Another striking characteristic of primitive ideology is the way in which so much of it is expressed in artistic, mostly ritual form. The usual art forms in a hunting-gathering society—myth, ritual, song and dance, and the less prevalent graphic arts—are themselves strikingly formalized on the one hand and largely, if not universally, confined to a supernaturalistic context. In fact, these characteristics of primitive life suggest that possibly the very origin of art is related to the widespread supernaturalistic context of existential beliefs. Art-making apparently began as an aspect of man's attempt to control nature and society by supernatural means, and it is probably for this reason that it is so highly ritualized.

We see, therefore, that in the aspects of ideology that we ordinarily think of as highly institutionalized, such as religion, science, codes of morality and ethics, or even the highly professionalized art-making of our society, the primitive manifestations stand in greatest contrast. In no case have the hunting-gathering societies clearly differentiated and institutionalized any aspect of culture and behavior above the familistic level. That is why it is difficult at any time to say just what actions of hunters and gatherers are economic or political or religious, or even artistic.

This unspecialized characteristic of primitive society results in one especially important contrast to modern civilization. It means that an individual adult participates much more fully in every aspect of the culture than do the people of more complicated societies. The concomitant for the human personality is that, because of the intimately social context in which everything is carried out, human beings in primitive society are personalized and individuated.[1] It sounds paradoxical to say, as we have from time to time, that band societies are strongly egalitarian and now to stress the individuation of their personnel. When we say a primitive society is egalitarian, we mean that it is strongly resistant to direction through authoritarian power of any kind. But within these societies the individual persons are not equal in the sense of being similar to one another. Each person is different from every other in terms of purely personal physical and psychological characteristics, as well as in statuses such as age, sex, marital state, and so on. Even in economic life there are no classes or categories of rich or poor, white-collar or laborer, skilled or unskilled people. This or that *person* is whatever he is, relatively skilled at some particular task, unskilled at another, or whatever.

The individuation of the person in primitive life is the antithesis of what has been called individualism, rugged or otherwise, in modern society. Our own individualism is related to the mechanical separation of persons from one another through specialization in labor and education, the breaking up of family communalism, and the increasing separation of the nuclear family from others. There is an increasing standardization and "togetherness," within the classes and occupations, while at the same time there is an increasing loneliness. Here is the paradox as Diamond puts it: "Rationalized, mechanized, and secularized civilization tends to produce standard and modal, rather than natural varieties of persons. The individual is always in danger of dissolving into the function or the status. . . . Yet it is precisely this kind of 'individualism' that inhibits the growth of the indivisible persons, that inner union of contraries. To paraphrase Erich Kahler, the history of civilization could very well be written as a history of the alienation of man." [2]

---

[1] See the interesting development of this point by Stanley Diamond, "The Search for the Primitive." In *Man's Image in Medicine and Anthropology*, ed. I. G. Gladston (New York: International Universities Press, 1963), pp. 62–115.

[2] *Ibid.*, pp. 104–105.

Appendix

In the following pages we have described separately the scattered hunting-gathering societies that constitute the sample from which this book has drawn its generalizations. The book necessarily emphasizes the functionally convergent traits, the basic similarities, that the societies share. But it seems sensible at this point to give some attention to the most important divergent adaptations, the dissimilarities, among the various groups. Thus a broad formulation of band society as a type now gives way to some specifics. These are real societies of real people, and this atlas-like account, however succinct, should serve to dispel some of the vagueness that inevitably is suggested by generalities.

The Eskimos

Before the Eskimos were decimated by commonplace European diseases against which they had had no immunity (even the common cold was a terrible killer), the population numbered about 100,000, spread across the Arctic of North America and Greenland. The population density was thus very thin. But it was also very uneven—some villages numbered hundreds of people in areas where whaling was good; others, only a few related families.

The Eskimos were completely dependent on game and fish and in this respect were unique among hunting-gathering societies, most of whom rely on vegetable food much more than on game. Caribou in spring and fall, fish in summer, and sea mammals—seal especially—in winter, were the Eskimos' main sources of food. The winter is very long and very cold, of course, and thus makes possible the preservation of meat and fish. Were this not the case the Eskimos could not have subsisted without vegetable foods, for game and fish can be acquired only sporadically, often in considerable abundance, to be sure, but also sometimes not at all over long periods of time.

Eskimo culture was similar throughout the Arctic, differing only so much as hunting methods differed. The Polar Eskimos of northern Greenland, for example, were almost completely adjusted to fishing and the hunting of sea mammals. The so-called Caribou Eskimos of the Canadian Barren Grounds, on the other hand, became independent of the sea and followed an inland hunting-fishing cycle. Others, the majority, blended caribou hunting and summer inland fishing with the winter hunting of sea mammals. The Copper Eskimos of the Central Canadian Arctic are the best-described example of this type.

Eskimos with dog sled. It is this kind of equipment which Arctic explorers have found irreplaceable. (Fujihara from Monkmeyer Press Photo Service.)

Today there are only about 36,000 Eskimos left, but it seems likely that their numbers will increase. Nowadays, they have more immunity to infectious diseases and even some medical care. Missions, schools, and governmental agencies in Greenland, Canada, and Alaska all afford some protection and educational adjustments to modern life.

Technology. The Eskimos had a much more ingenious and elaborate technology than any of the other hunting-gathering societies we have covered in this book. Many of these items are so useful in the Arctic that modern exploring expeditions have found them irreplaceable. We need mention only the well-known sledges and dog teams, igloos, kayaks, fur snow boots, parkas, snow goggles, and so on, to make this point. Joined harpoons, usually used in sealing, were so well-made that they were often used for hunting the much larger walrus and even the whale. Given the scarcity of wood and absence of metalworking (although the Copper Eskimos cold-hammered copper nuggets into crude knives and choppers) the Eskimos were very adept at making a large variety of implements out of bone, stone, and ivory. Particularly impressive are such delicate articles as needles, combs, awls, spoons, and highly artistic figurines, all cut, shaped, and decorated with a rotary bow drill. Hunting weapons were considerably varied, as might be expected. They included the bow and arrow, many kinds of lances, fish spears, and numerous harpoons. Household utensils included soapstone lamp bowls (for burning seal blubber) and pots for boiling meat, sealskin cups, bags, buckets, and storage bags.

Economy and Society. It is impossible to generalize about the size or complexity of Eskimo communities because some were large at certain seasons of the year and fragmented at others (usually in the summer), and most also varied greatly during the history of their relations with the white man. As remarked above, however, in aboriginal times whaling was an important industry for nearly all the coastal communities and some of these were very large—as many as 500 permanent residents—which contrasts greatly with the other communities we have considered in this book.

All the basic economic tasks and specialities were undertaken by the individual family. Exchanges of goods involved the simple sharing of surpluses among families. The relative self-sufficiency of each family and the seasonal shifts of residence affected the pattern of kinship. The Eskimos were not all alike in this respect, but in most communities true siblings were distinguished from cousins, who were not differentiated into cross and parallel varieties, just as in the usual English-speaker's habit. Mother and father were distinguished from their brothers and sisters, and own children were distinguished from brothers' and sisters' children. However logical this may seem to us, it is nevertheless unusual in the primitive world, for ordinarily the nuclear family is not so independent.

Life is precarious in the Arctic and late winter famine is sometimes a threat, as it also is sometimes when people are forced to travel long distances in the winter. This situation led the Eskimos to infanticide and the miscalled "mercy killing" of the aged. In this latter case, it was often the aged who insisted on their abandonment or who, if they were able, would take their own lives when the family was threatened.

Polity. The Eskimo communities were small, usually, and were governed by rules of behavior that were essentially familistic rather than by explicit law and government of the formal, institutionalized type. Leadership, when above the paternal level in a nuclear family, was charismatic—that is, a man tended to rise to a position of esteem and thus to leadership in some one kind of enterprise by his past performances. But it was never an overweening kind of personal *power*, only the kind of personal authority that can come from the community's appreciation of his past efforts.

The adjudication of quarrels, likewise, was not the prerogative of some official, but was affected through the action of kin groups and public opinion. Often, when there was no clearly defined public opinion manifested, some kind of duel between the accuser and accused would be arranged so that the onlookers could encourage the person they favored. This was a way of arriving at a consensus by making at least some opinion manifest at the outset. The duels were often wrestling, boxing, or headbutting contests. More widespread, and certainly more famous, were the unique song-duels. A favorite form of entertainment, the duel of two persons who took turns in singing little extemporaneous songs insulting the other were used to allow the public to manifest its favor for one of the contestants.

Ideology. Eskimo ideology was similar to that of other very primitive peoples. Its existential knowledge was largely cast in supernatural terms and its normative values formally phrased, ordinarily as etiquette.

Supernaturalism, as spiritism, was the salient feature of the ideology. Everything in the cosmos was imbued with supernatural force. Even the individual pebbles on the beach had their own souls. Some of the spirits were significant enough to be classed as gods when they offered means of control over something significant to the Eskimos' lives. Sedna, for example, was a former human being who became goddess of the sea mammals. She had the power to withhold game from humans unless various rituals were properly observed.

Taboos on various forms of activity governed much of everyday life. These were the ritual means of keeping the various ghosts and spirits from continually doing harm. Perhaps the most noticeable as well as widespread taboo had to do with the separation of all activities having to do with land animals from those having to do with sea mammals. Thus an Eskimo was not permitted to sew skins of caribou, a land animal, while camped on the ice.

Selected Readings. Kaj Birket-Smith, *The Eskimos* (London: Methuen, 1959) is a general book on the Eskimos by one of the greatest authorities on the Arctic. In Peter Freuchen, *Book of the Eskimo* (Cleveland, New

York: World Publishing Co., 1961) are found some highly personalized anecdotes about this Danish explorer's many years in Greenland. Diamond Jenness, *The People of the Twlight* (Chicago: University of Chicago Press, 1959) recounts his adventures among the Copper Eskimos between the years 1913 and 1918.

Knut Rasmussen, *Across Arctic America* (London, New York: Putnam and Sons, 1927) is a general account of Eskimo culture by one of the greatest of Arctic authorities, based on his extensive travels. Hans Ruesch, *Top of the World* (New York: Harper and Brothers, 1950 and Pocket Books, 1951) is a fictional treatment of Eskimo life in northern Greenland which is accurate and interesting. Vilhjalmur Stefansson, *My Life with the Eskimos* (New York: The Macmillan Company, 1919) was written for the general public by the famous American explorer of the Canadian Arctic. More of the same sort of materials is found in his later book, *The Friendly Arctic* (New York: The Macmillan Company, 1921). A detailed comparative study and general summing up of Eskimo culture can be found in Edward Weyer, *The Eskimos: Their Environment and Folkways* (New Haven: Yale University Press, 1932).

The Algonkian and Athabascan Hunters of Canada

Most of the extensive forests of aboriginal Canada south of the Eskimos' area was inhabited by Indian hunters. Those roughly to the east and south of Hudson's Bay spoke Algonkian. (The best-known of these are the Montagnais-Naskapi in Labrador and the Chippewa—or Ojibwa—in Ontario.) The central and western Canadian Indians spoke Athabascan. (Those of the simple hunting level include Hare, Dogrib, Bear Lake, Yellowknife, Chipewyan, Mountain, Kaska, Slave, Sekani, and Beaver.)

In aboriginal times these two groups of Indians were probably much alike, with the main cultural differences occurring along an axis from north to south, rather than from east to west. In both the Algonkian and Athabascan area the greatest difference in habitat was from the northern tundra, or Barren Grounds, to the forests that are progressively more dense and heavy with game toward the south. The primary subsistence resource was large game. In the north, caribou and muskoxen were the most important; and in the forests, deer, small buffalo (in the west), and many kinds of smaller game such as beaver and rabbits were hunted and trapped. Summer fishing was extremely important for most of the Indians in both north and south.

In most of sub-Arctic Canada, population was less dense than in the Eskimo area. The agglomerations of people depended, of course, on the resources of the area and the time of year. In some zones, large numbers concentrated around the lakes where the fishing was good. In winter the communities were very small, the people foraging widely for small game. In fall and spring, again, many might prey on the migrating caribou.

Athabascan hunter of the Canadian Yukon bringing in a load of wood. The conical shaped tent is made of skins. (Black Star.)

Technology. Despite living in a similarly bitter winter environment, the Canadian Indians differed from the Eskimo in many ways, even in clothing, housing, and other forms of technological adaptation to the harsh environment. Conical skin tents and more permanent double lean-tos of bark replaced the igloos. Toboggans were used instead of dog sleds, and moccasins were worn rather than sealskin boots. Snowshoes, birch-bark canoes, bark cooking vessels (in which food was boiled by dropping hot stones into the water), snares and nets for small game, and the bow and arrow were other characterstic items.

Economy and Society. Nothing is known about details of the purely aboriginal social organization, for all these Indians were much affected by the fur-trading companies at a very early date, long before we have any reliable descriptions (for this is not the kind of thing that is described in the documents left by early traders and explorers). First, the unfamiliar European diseases took a terrible toll. One single smallpox epidemic in the 1780s nearly wiped out the aboriginal population of all of Canada. Those who survived quickly became employees, or debtor-workers, of the fur-trading companies and their aboriginal way of life became, of course, completely altered. Rifles and steel traps were taken in exchange for furs, and finally canvas tents, stoves, European clothing and food (and inevitably tobacco and alcohol) were used as the men became more and more occupied as full-time workers. The social organization above the level of the nuclear family was shattered, and the economic system was reduced mostly to the individual activities of trappers.

Polity. It may be presumed that in aboriginal times the forms of leadership and authority above the level of the individual family were of the sort we have earlier called charismatic. Certainly this was the case later, after the Indians had re-adapted to the fur trade. During these later days, however, leadership was more firmly established because the traders dealt indirectly with most of the Indians, funneling the goods and receiving the furs through some particular individuals adjudged to be leaders. This, of course, made the would-be leader much more solidly and permanently entrenched in his position. Nevertheless, the leader could not subjugate his people at will. There seemed to be an active aversion toward any kind of authority that moved beyond influence toward subjugation.

Influential persons sometimes offered an opinion that helped adjudicate quarrels, but this was rare. There was no official status outside the kinship system for such conduct. And it would have been, perforce, rather dangerous for someone aspiring to power to risk interfering. The Athabascans are said to have admired certain personal qualities—hard work, being a good provider, supernatural powers above the average, wisdom, generosity—but "in the Dené view the will to power *per se* is not conceived to be admirable or socially desirable. The reaction to this will when encountered nakedly is not just indifferent, it is negative." [1]

Ideology. Supernaturalism among the Canadian Indians resembled that of the Eskimos. The shaman and his spirit-helper performed the usual conjuring tricks to heal sick or injured persons, much as did the *angakok* of the Eskimos. One procedure of the Algonkian Indians of Canada was unusual in its particulars, although it resembled the widespread use of spirit-helpers in predicting the future. The device used was the so-called shaking-tent, a small lodge in which the diviner was placed, bound hand and foot. A gust of wind would shake the lodge as strange sounds began to come from within, a sign the spirit-helpers had come and were speaking through the lips of the diviner, answering questions posed by the surrounding audience. When the séance was over, it was found that the diviner had been freed of his bonds as a sign of the power of the unseen visitors.

As in many other societies that lack political institutions, a shaman may

---

[1] June Helm MacNeish, "Leadership among the Northeastern Athabascans." *Anthropologica*, No. 2 (1956), 154.

inspire fear because of his unusual control of supernatural power. His role becomes, in addition to curing and perhaps predicting the future, that of a possible sorcerer. After all, if one has extraordinary power to heal people, could he not have extraordinary power to harm? Among Indians of the upper Great Lakes region, there was an organization of shamans called the *Mide*, who not only pooled their specialized talents and kept them secret like a kind of guild, but also used their occult powers to frighten and coerce people (and in more modern times to restrict competition and maintain high fees).

Selected Readings. Diamond Jenness, *Indians of Canada* (Ottawa: National Museum of Canada, Bulletin 65, 1932) is a very general descriptive survey by a modern authority on the Canadian Indians. A short monograph by Eleanor Leacock, "The Montagnais 'Hunting Territory' and the Fur Trade," *American Anthropological Association Memoir*, No. 78, n. d., uses modern ethnological materials to supplement early historical documents to show how the European fur trade altered the social and economic organization of the Algonkian Indians in Canada. Her bibliography is an excellent guide to earlier studies by Frank Speck and others.

June Helm MacNeish, "Leadership among the Northeastern Athabascans," *Anthropologica*, No. 2 (1956), is a particularly useful discussion of the nature of political organization both under aboriginal conditions and after the fur trade had become established. A missionary who spent much of his life among the Athabascans (*Dené*) in western Canada, Father A. G. Morice, became a recognized ethnological authority on them with the publication of his "The Great Dené Race," *Anthropos*, Vols. 1, 2, 4, 5 (1906, 1907, 1909, 1910).

The Indians
of the Great Basin

The Great Basin is the huge region between the Sierra Nevadas and the Rocky Mountains, including the states of Nevada, western Utah, parts of eastern California, and the northwestern corner of Arizona. Prior to the use of horses, the whole area was peopled by similar hunting-gathering Indians, largely of Shoshonean speech. In the nineteenth century, some of the eastern and northern Indians of the Basin became equestrian and are known now as Utes. In the central arid part of the Basin, the Indians now called Paiute and Western Shoshone continued their peaceful hunting-gathering on foot until most of them were finally placed on reservations in the 1870s.

The Great Basin is a steppe-like near-desert, with uplands and mountains at its edges which cause distinct vegetational zones. The migrations of the people and the size of their occasional agglomerations were related to the seasonal fluctuations of food in these various zones. Large game was scarce; more important were rodents, especially rabbits, insects, grass seeds, roots, berries, and the piñon nuts from the uplands in autumn. All of these items are rather poor provender compared to the abundance offered the people of the tropical forests, but an important feature of arid lands is the fact that most of the above items are storable, whereas the wet climate of the forest and the emphasis on fruit and meat preclude storage.

The population was necessarily small and scattered, with the average density about 1 person to 15.6 square miles. The central desert, of course, was least inhabited (1 person to 30 or 40 square miles), while in the foothills near rivers much larger communities could gather.

Technology. Rude bows and arrows, spears, and a throwing stick for killing small game were the usual weapons. Housing consisted of small conical brush huts that contained the nuclear family. Clothing was sparse; moccasins and loincloth in summer supplemented by a rabbit cloak in winter comprised the normal wardrobe. Because of the considerable seasonal contrasts, techniques of food storage were extremely important. Grass seeds were stored and transported in skin bags, as were pine nuts by the people in the vicinity of the uplands where the piñon grew. Grasshoppers were pounded into a paste and berries were dried, as was the rarer meat in some instances. Underground pits were dug at the winter quarters as caches for these items. The most highly refined craft of the Shoshone was basketry, mostly made of split willow twigs. Some were proofed with hot pitch and made into vessels in which food was boiled by heated stones dropped into the water.

Economy and Society. Seasonal and geographic variations in the amount and kinds of foods available required a considerable nomadism and corresponding variations in the size of the agglomerations of people. During the spring and summer, individual families were scattered alone or in the company of only a few close relatives simply because the foods sought at those times—seeds, roots, small rodents, grasshoppers—were themselves so dispersed. But in winter, the pine-nut harvest was sometimes so plentiful that twenty or thirty families could live together on the accumulated reserve of nuts.

The food supply was so unpredictable that the migrations of the people could not be confined to consistent routes or within conventional territories. Hence, less than among most hunting-gathering societies, neither bands nor individual families exercised permanent rights to territories. J. H. Steward, the foremost ethnologist of the Shoshone, believed that these conditions must have prevented the formation of recognized bands of people with kinship based on band exogamy. There was, however, evidence of cross-cousin marriage.

The infrequency of large gatherings of people did not result in any apparent lack of sociability when they did gather together. Dances were especially popular and gambling games were very numerous, including several forms of dice.

Polity. Leadership in normal times was merely familistic, as might be expected, considering the small size of the groups. Sometimes a concerted rabbit drive would include numerous families, and in such cases it was conventional for one person to be recognized as the "rabbit boss" who would coordinate the movements of the people.

In aboriginal times the Shoshone were not warlike. It was not until the acquisition of the horse from the Spanish that some of them became predatory bands of raiders. (These Indians are now called Utes and are distinguished from the unmounted Shoshone.) Feud, rather than warfare, had been the more usual form of inter-band hostility.

Ideology. The most usual feuds stemmed from the suspicion of witchcraft being practiced. Death was thought to be the result of supernatural causes, and often a malign shaman would be blamed. He would, of course, be from another group, and if he were killed by the aggrieved his death would be likely to call forth counter-measures, with a full-scale feud the probable result.

There was no organized priesthood and very little occasion for group religious activities. Contact with the supernatural was largely an individual concern. Dances were held when it was possible for people to congregate, but these seem to have been primarily recreational with only a slight amount of supernatural content.

Selected Readings. Julian H. Steward, *Basin-Plateau Aboriginal Sociopolitical Groups* (Washington, D.C.: Smithsonian Institution Bureau of American Ethnology, Bulletin 120, 1938) is the standard monograph on the Shoshonean hunters and gatherers of the western desert. See also Steward's interpretive book, particularly chapters 6, 7, and 8, *Theory of Culture Change* (Urbana: University of Illinois Press, 1955).

The Indians
of Tierra del Fuego

The large island of Tierra del Fuego offers two contrasting kinds of food resources. The littoral is rich in shellfish, especially mussels, and fish, seals, water birds, and now and then a beached whale. The inland plains (in earlier times) were productive primarily of herds of wild guanaco, a species of small camel peculiar to South America. These two kinds of resources were exploited by nomadic Indians who, in adapting to them, became quite different from each other in certain respects.

The coastal Indians best known to us are the Yahgan. Nearby were the Alakaluf, and further north along the Chilean archipelago, the little-known Chono. All were apparently much alike in aboriginal times, but they are now nearly extinct and the survivors are considerably acculturated. The Yahgan numbered about 3,000 in the 1880s when they were studied by Rev. Thomas Bridges, a resident missionary.

The Ona Indians were the inland hunters (also studied by Rev. Bridges). About 2,000 of them occupied a territory of some 20,000 square miles. The southern plains of Argentina were also occupied by Ona-like hunters before the coming of Spaniards. Only a few Ona survived the European diseases.

Technology. The Yahgan and the Ona differ strikingly in their form of technological adaptation to the resources they exploited. The Yahgan spent so much time in their canoes, fishing and gathering shellfish, that they have been called the "canoe Indians," as opposed to the "foot Indians," the Ona. The Yahgan women were the shellfish gatherers and the men specialized in fishing and bird hunting. The Ona women, on the other hand, had no important occupation because of the relative absence of wild foods to be gathered in their territory.

Housing was crude among both groups of Indians. The more permanent huts were of a conical shape made by piling branches and brush around a central pole. The more nomadic Indians of the plains made simple lean-tos of guanaco skins, in the fashion of the Patagonians. Crude moccasins and heavy, cumbersome cloaks of sealskin were their only clothing. Weapons were bows and arrows, spears, and harpoons (used by the Yahgan).

Economy and Society. The Ona nuclear family was part of a patrilocal band that was well-defined in terms of the territory that it defended against trespassers. The Yahgan, however, were so scattered over so complicated a coastline that it is difficult to say whether they had territorial boundaries or not. If a patrilocal band of the Ona type ever existed, it had disappeared through decimation of the population at the time they were studied.

Both Ona and Yahgan prohibited marriage with close relatives, but only the Ona were exogamous in terms of territorial boundaries. Monogamy was usual with both. No bride price or bride service was required. Exchange of goods was entirely in terms of kinship reciprocity and apparently was quite informal and general.

Polity. Authority was entirely familistic, and there seem to have been no formal ways of publicly adjudicating quarrels. There was no organized warfare, and injuries were simply subject to retaliation if they involved unrelated groups.

Ideology. The most notable departure of the Fuegian ideology from the usual hunting-gathering bands was with respect to a myth perpetuated by the men's secret society. This myth was associated with the ceremony that initiated adolescent boys into manhood. The main ingredients in the ceremony were physical ordeals, and then the imparting of the lore that was kept secret from women and children. The myth was essentially that once women ruled the men, but that finally men banded together into a society that used secret rituals to gain the supernatural power that women had monopolized by impersonating spirits. The women were finally overthrown in a great battle. During the ceremony itself, both Ona and Yahgan used the masked spirit impersonators whose identity was revealed only to the initiated boys. The climax of the ceremony was a mock battle that recapitulated the defeat of the women.

Other aspects of the mythology and ritualism differed only in detail from the usual life-cycle ceremonies and the curing shamanism of the previously described Indian hunting-gathering societies.

Selected Readings. E. Lucas Bridges, *Uttermost Part of the Earth* (New York: E. P. Dutton, 1949) is a reminiscence of his childhood in Tierra del Fuego at his father's mission for Ona and Yahgan Indians. The book contains many interesting anecdotes and photographs. John M. Cooper, "The Yahgan" in J. H. Steward, ed., *Handbook of South American Indians*, Vol. 1 (Washington, D.C.: Smithsonian Institution Bureau of American Ethnology, Bulletin 143, Government Printing Office, 1946) is a summary of the scattered literature on the Yahgan.

Father Martin Gusinde, *Die Feuerland-Indianer*, 2 Vols. (Modling bie Wien: Verlag Der Internationalen Zeitschrift "Anthropos," 1931) is the basic ethnological account of the Fuegians. Volume 1 is about the Ona and Volume 2, the Yahgan. Volume 2 has been translated into English for the Human Relations Area Files. Samuel K. Lothrop, "Indians of Tierra del Fuego," *Contributions*, Museum of the American Indian, Vol. 10 (New York: Heye Foundation, 1928), is a summary of Ona and Yahgan culture based on personal interviews with the few surviving Indians during the middle 1920s.

The Pygmies
of the African Congo

The Ituri Forest covers many thousands of square miles of the tropical lowland in the northeast corner of the Zaire. The climate is equatorial, with the temperatures ranging daily between 70 and 90 degrees F. throughout the year. In this dense, rainy jungle in almost the exact middle of Africa range small groups of Pygmies in their search for food. Some of the game hunted is of monster size—elephants, hippopotamus, and buffalos—as well as various kinds of antelope and wild pigs. An important part of the subsistence is also provided by the women, who gather mushrooms, nuts, roots, fruits, and grubs.

Some of the hunters have close symbiotic relations with their Bantu-speaking agricultural neighbors. Surplus meat is exchanged for corn beer and handicrafts, and it is said that the agriculturalists also extend their protection to the hunters. But many other Pygmies who live in the more interior forests have little to do with outsiders, remaining self-sufficient in the food quest as well as in their arts and crafts.

These latter, the independent Pygmies called the BaMbuti, number about 40,000. Of all the Pygmies, these have been able best to resist the influences of the Bantu as well as modern civilization. Turnbull's book, the source for the present précis, is an account of their culture as it exists today.

Technology. The most unusual device of the BaMbuti is the hunting net that many of the family heads employ for entangling large game. These nets are long (100 to 300 feet) and about 4 feet wide. Spears are used for killing the trapped game. Bows and poisoned arrows are used in hunting small game and birds.

Housing consists of small beehive-shaped huts of brush and leaves. Clothing is minimal, mostly a simple loincloth made of bark cloth. Food is roasted over an open fire, but some wild vegetables and fruits are mashed in a wooden mortar. Inasmuch as the camps are rather more permanent than those of most hunting peoples—the BaMbuti average about a month in the same camp—they are inclined to fix the houses a little more carefully and even to make simple chairs and bed frames.

Economy and Society. The forest feeds the Pygmies without a great deal of effort on their part. The men go off to hunt the great variety of game while the women gather in a short time the numerous varieties of mushrooms, nuts, roots, and fruits, which are never far away. The supply is so constant (for there are no seasons) and abundant that there is no need to store food in anticipation of a lean or unlucky time. Exchanges of goods are informal and frequent, but there is no standard bride price or service. Those who live near the Bantu settlements give meat for bananas, corn beer, manioc, and tobacco.

The settlements consist of at least six or seven individual families, for that is the minimum number of males who can properly form a hunting group. Some of the game is so large that very careful cooperation between those men is an absolute requirement. The bands are exogamous, with the preference to "marry far," as they say. However, the relations between bands are so normally peaceful and exogamy has created such a wide network of related peoples among them that people sometimes change their band affiliation. When this happens frequently enough, the band becomes somewhat composite and marriages can take place within it. But usually, even today, the young men seek their mates from families that live in distant groups.

A marriage ceremony lays an obligation on the groom's band to provide a suitable girl later on for a boy of the wife's band. (This is sometimes called "sister exchange" by anthropologists, but it must be understood that "sister" is used in the broadest classificatory sense.)

Polity.   The bands have no formal chiefs or councils of elders who make decisions. An important man might take the lead in an argument about what is to be done, but public consensus is required before any action is taken.

Ideology.   The Pygmies are skilled at singing, dancing, and miming. The subject is always about the forest and their own relation to it, usually in terms of the hunt.

Curing shamanism and life-cycle ceremonies are not greatly different from those of other hunting-gathering peoples. Boys' initiation is by far the most prominent of the ceremonies, involving much ritual, public circumcision, and other ordeals that may continue for as long as six weeks. It has been said by some (but denied by Turnbull) that this ceremony, as well as many other traits, was borrowed from the Bantu villagers. The original Pygmy language, for example, has disappeared and the Pygmies all speak the Bantu language of their neighbors, even among themselves.

Selected Readings.   Paul Schebesta, *Among Congo Pygmies* (London: Hutchinson and Co., 1933) is a standard ethnological account of the Pygmies. Colin M. Turnbull, *The Forest People* (New York: Simon and Schuster, 1961) is written by an anthropologist, but it is not in the standardized ethnological form. Much as Mrs. Thomas did in *The Harmless People*, Dr. Turnbull personalizes the culture with anecdotes about particular individuals.

The Bushmen
of South Africa

The aboriginal hunting population of South Africa, which once covered the whole southern third of Africa, succumbed to slow intrusions by Bantu agriculturalists on both their eastern and western flanks long before the coming of Europeans to South Africa. In more modern times the Europeans also have taken up desirable land, so that the Bushmen hunters still practice their ancient way of life in only two inhospitable areas in the southwest, the Kalahari Desert and the Okavango Swamp region. Some of the !Kung Bushmen of the desert, the least acculturated of surviving Bushmen, have been recently studied and will be the specific Bushmen referred to in the following précis.

The total number of !Kung is about 4,000, but those who still follow the ancient hunting way of life on a year-round basis number only a few bands, scattered very widely over the arid wastes. In utter contrast to the Pygmies of the Ituri Forest, the !Kung are a hungry people, their habits oriented around a constant struggle for food and water. Vegetable foods are rare most of the year, as is grass and water that would attract game; hence the Bushmen band is almost constantly migrating. The most usual game hunted is a small antelope, birds, rodents, snakes, insects, lizards, and the difficult ostrich. Foods gathered include mostly roots and seeds, and in the northern areas fruits and nuts.

Technology. The bow and poisoned arrows, spears, and clubs are the main hunting weapons. During the hot season big game is sometimes simply run down, chased at a steady, relentless trot until the animal drops from exhaustion. Roots are dug by women with a sharpened digging stick. The stomach of large animals is used for storing water, as are ostrich eggshells. These shells are also used for manufacturing beads, which form the most important article of barter among many Bushmen.

A most important factor in the Bushman's struggle for survival is the search for water. Detailed knowledge of the geography is of course to be expected, but in addition the Bushmen know how to find subterranean water and after digging until moisture is encountered they suck the water out through a reed that has a glass filter in the bottom. Rainwater is caught in ostrich eggshells.

Housing varies in size and shape in the various regions. The simplest is merely a semicircular shelter of branches stuck into the ground and covered with grass, perhaps no more than 4 feet high. In more permanent camps, the hut may be made larger and completed into a dome shape.

Economy and Society. Scarcity of food has resulted in a rather extreme emphasis on rules of sharing. The sharing is formalized and ritualized, and fortified by the belief that any deviation in the procedure would result in the failure of the poisons to act in future hunts.

The division of labor between men and women is strictly observed. Men hunt, make weapons, and prepare skins for clothing, while women do all the gathering of vegetable foods and small burrowing game and insects, build the huts, gather wood and build the fire, cook, and keep the camp clean.

The northern Bushmen (the least acculturated) once were grouped into patrilocal, exogamous bands, about twenty persons per band; but the !Kung in modern times are not so formal about their marital residence practices. Temporary uxorilocal residence of about a year (or until the first child is born) is frequent, as are levirate and sororate. The kinship terminology does not distinguish cross from parallel cousins, and in modern times is usually the Hawaiian (or "generational," as it is sometimes called). An unusual intrusion of personal naming customs may be responsible for this. Every person is named after some relative and is referred to by a kinship term which indicates his namesake's relationship to ego rather than his own. The !Kung also consider all kinship terms to be in one of two major categories, referring to relatives to whom formal behavior must obtain and those with whom one must joke (that is, behave with extreme informality).

Polity. The bands are sometimes said to have a "big man" or chief, but although he may be influential in many ways, he has no real power over anyone. Inter-band relations are peacefully conducted between bands that contain relatives, but strange bands are feared and avoided.

Ideology. The precariousness of the food supply is matched by a great number of supernatural precautions about the conduct of the hunt and the sharing of meat. Shamanism, and the corollary belief in sorcery by malign shamans, is also common among Bushmen, as among all other hunting-gathering peoples.

The Bushmen are very fond of music, singing, and the dance. A usual instrument for accompanying singing is simply a hunting bow, played like a single-stringed viol, with one end resting on a hollow gourd that serves as a sound box. Except for medicine songs, the Bushmen sing "mood songs," songs without words, composed in order to express a mood or emotion. They may also dance for enjoyment rather than as a magical ritual, although they also have curing, or medicine, dances. Life-cycle ceremonies are modest and unpeculiar, with the single exception of initiation, wherein all male neophytes are given secret medicine lore. All men, therefore, are potential curing shamans, but inasmuch as some are better at it than others, the more skillful tend to practice their art more frequently.

Selected Readings. L. Marshall, *The !Kung of the Nyae-Nyae* (Cambridge: Harvard University Press, 1976) is the most detailed and complete ethnographic account of !Kung Bushmen life. R. B. Lee and I. Devore (eds.) *The Kalahari Hunter-Gatherers* (Cambridge: Harvard University Press, 1976) contains a number of detailed articles on !Kung life by members of the Harvard University research project. E. M. Thomas, *The Harmless People* (New York: Knopf, 1959) is a well-written anecdotal account of her experiences among the Bushmen.

The Australians

The Australian continent, approximating the area of the United States of America, contained about 300,000 people before the coming of Europeans. This modest population was very unevenly distributed over the landscape because of the diversity in kinds and amounts of food available for exploitation by a simple hunting-gathering technology. Some of the tropical coastal areas were lush in edible vegetation and rich in game and fish. In the interior deserts, however, nature is niggardly and the small bands were widely separated. Accordingly, the coastal people hunted more, and with greater success, than the desert people, who depended much more on collecting sparse vegetable food, rodents, reptiles, and insects.

Despite the considerable differences in the demographic makeup of these societies and the variation in the degree of nomadism imposed on them by the natural distribution of food, there was a surprising similarity in the culture of all of the Australian natives.

Today there are only about 50,000 aborigines left. In southwestern Australia, the area of earliest and greatest European settlement, the natives have long since vanished, and they are declining rapidly in the central and western zones. Only in Arnhem land in the tropical north and in the Kimberly country of the northwest are there many remaining who live the old free life of nomadic hunters.

Technology. The Australian kit of weapons differs from the others discussed so far in the absence of the bow and arrow and in the presence of

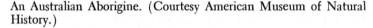

An Australian Aborigine. (Courtesy American Museum of Natural History.)

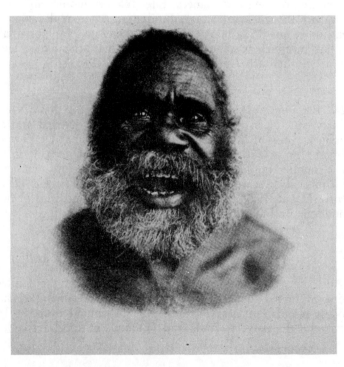

the unique boomerang. The spear is used with a spear-thrower, which is occasionally found among hunting-gathering peoples. The Australians have many varieties of throwing sticks, some heavy with a sharp edge, some light for throwing at birds. But the boomerang that does tricks in the air, hovering or returning, is more or less a plaything, used in hunting only for throwing into a flock of birds. Nets, traps, snares, and pitfalls are also used in hunting.

Flint implements vary greatly, depending on whether they are used for cutting, chopping, abrading, adzing, or boring. The women use a sharpened stick for digging roots, and a wooden or bark trough-like device and nets for transporting the produce. Culinary arts are simple; food is baked in ashes or simply roasted directly on the fire.

The huts are usually small, domed, single-family edifices made of a frame of branches covered with leaves, grass, reeds—whatever is available. They use no furniture nor wear any clothing, nor even any kind of bed covering. Sometimes the nights are bitterly cold, but the people merely keep the fire going and sleep crowded around it.

Economy and Society. As among all primitive peoples, food is shared by principles of reciprocity, and at certain occasions gifts are given among classes of relatives with great formality, especially at weddings. Goods are also exchanged in formal reciprocity among adjacent bands so that some goods, mostly raw materials of limited distribution, are passed along trade routes for hundreds of miles.

The size of the bands varies from as many as two or more hundred people in the coastal areas to as small as twenty or thirty in the arid interior. Normally the bands migrate in a region recognized as their own home country, although they may also freely penetrate the territory of neighboring bands, who are often related in some way. The bands are patrilocal in composition, in consequence of the virilocal marital residence custom. Cross-cousin marriage is preferred, and sometimes the rule prescribes second (or proscribes first) cross-cousin marriage.

Some of the Australian bands are unusual in the primitive world in having named categories of relatives who reflect the kinship system but exist independently of it. These are the so-called marriage classes, more recently called the section system (if four categories are named) or the subsection (if eight). It could also be said that they have a two-class system in that very frequently Australian societies are divided into two parts which intermarry. This, however, is very common in the primitive world and is called the moiety system. The four-class system is simply a moiety system subdivided by distinguishing the adjacent generations; eight by a further subdivision which makes "semi-moieties" by separating first cross cousins from the others in both moieties—a distinction that is found only in those societies that prohibit marriage with the first cross cousins.

Polity. The Australians are sometimes said to be ruled as a gerontocracy. This is because the elder men are treated with great respect and because they sometimes "sit" as a sort of council to adjudicate disputes. Sometimes feuds are prevented and quarrels settled by "expiatory encounters." (See p. 55 in text.) Warfare is simply an act of revenge perpetrated by one group for an injury by another. It seldom results in much bloodshed and never involves taking land or any other possessions.

Ideology. Curing shamans and the related conceptions of sorcery are similar to those found among other hunting-gathering societies. One feature of the sorcerer's art may be unusual, however, This is the small "pointing-bone" which the sorcerer chants over, after which he can point it toward a victim, "sending" it magically into him to cause his death.

Perhaps the most unusually elaborated characteristics of Australian society are the totemic beliefs and rituals. All social groups—the bands, moieties, even the sexes—are believed to have descended from some particular plant or animal species, and each group is responsible for performing the magical ceremonies that promote the increase of the species. Thus in the absence of a true economic division of labor among the various groups, a ceremonial and ideological set of specializations creates an organic kind of social inter-dependence.

Of the life-crisis rites, the initiation of young boys is by far the most elaborate. As among other band societies, the ceremonies isolate the youths from the company of women and children and introduce them to the secret rites and sacred beliefs as well as to a code of discipline and rectitude maintained by the mature men. The initiates are tested by fire ordeals and ritual operations such as tooth-removal, scarification, and circumcision.

An important aspect of religion in Australia is the art of painting on bark, incising on stone, and wood carving. These sometimes may be media for sorcery, and for hunting, fishing, and love magic. Designs are usually geometric and invariable because they are actually ritual. Some designs endow the decorated object with the sacred power of the spirit world.

Selected Readings. A. P. Elkin, *The Australian Aborigines: How to Understand Them* (Sydney and London: Angus and Robertson, 1954) is a general authoritative account of the aborigines by the foremost Australian ethnologist. M. J. Meggitt, *Desert People* (Sydney: Angus and Robertson, 1962), is the first full-length study of a central Australian group since early in the century, and a very well-conceived monograph.

W. L. Warner, *A Black Civilization* (New York: Harper and Brothers, 1937) is an intensive study of the Murngin in northeastern Arnhem Land. The book furnishes a good contrast to the desert habitat of the Arunta, for the Murngin live in a rainier, tropical coastal region.

Baldwin Spencer and F. J. Gillen, *The Arunta* (Two Vols. London: The Macmillan Company, 1927) is an anthropological classic. The field work was done around the turn of the century, before the culture of the Arunta of the central Desert was seriously disturbed. The book is particularly famous for its depiction of Arunta religion. Spencer and Gillen also wrote *The Northern Tribes of Central Australia* (London: The Macmillan Company,

1899), and Spencer wrote *The Native Tribes of the Northern Territory of Australia* (London: The Macmillan Company, 1914).

The Semang
of the Malay Peninsula

The Semang live in the foothills and lower slopes of the interior mountain ranges of the Malay Peninsula in a tropical jungle of exceptionally heavy rainfall. They are of the pygmy Negro, usually called Negrito, stock and are believed to have been the earliest of the various inhabitants of Southern Asia.

The jungle is full of animal life, large and small, but the Semang, unlike the Congo Pygmies, hunt only rats, squirrels, birds, and lizards, and only rarely an animal as large as the pig. The most important elements of the diet are such vegetable foods as yams, berries, nuts, roots, leaves, shoots, and fruit, especially durian. Fish are important in some areas.

The Semang have always been helpless in their association with their Malayan neighbors and were always crowded out of any desired area by these more numerous farming people. The population of Semang has dwindled in modern times and the culture of the survivors is much altered toward that of the dominant Malay.

Technology. Bamboo is the most useful item in the forest for the Semang. Fire-hardened, its splinters make sharp knives, spear and arrow points, and as a tube it is used as a cooking vessel, arrow quiver, and water carrier. The bow and arrow tipped with poison is the main weapon.

Housing is very simple because the bands migrate so frequently. Rattan leaves are interlaced over a simple dome framework of light branches. Raised couches of bamboo are commonly the only furniture used. Clothing consists merely of a loincloth made by pounding the inner bark of the breadfruit tree.

Economy and Society. Sharing of food and general hospitality are important virtues of the Semang, as they are of the other primitive peoples we have studied. Only two economic practices are a little unusual. One is the "silent trade" whereby the Negritos leave some jungle products at a conventional place near a Malay village, coming later to find what has been left in return—usually salt, beads, and sometimes a metal tool such as a knife. The other peculiarity is the ownership by individuals of particular durian trees. The harvest is usually shared within the group, but it is considered improper to pick the fruit from a tree belonging to another person.

Semang bands are small, usually of no more than twenty to thirty people. Each roams within a recognized territory of some twenty square miles within which are the durian trees belonging to the adult male members. Inasmuch as the trees are inherited among males, father to son, the group is patrilocal, the wives coming from some other nearby band.

Within any larger territory there is a tendency for bands to continue intermarrying and to associate more consistently with one another than with certain others. Thus there are a few contiguous bands with a similarity in speech and customs that results in some sense of community, which in turn sets them off from others with whom communication has become increasingly difficult.

Polity. This larger entity is not organized politically, nor does it act consciously as a body. Only the component bands have any significant collective functions, and they are, of course, the residential groups. There is a tendency for the bands to follow the directions of the oldest man in the group, but this is a recognition of his greater wisdom rather than indicating any system of formal leadership or authority.

Ideology. As expected, the shaman is the most influential person in the band. Illness and death are caused by an evil spirit entering the body, and the shaman is the only one who knows how to exorcise it. The shaman also can become a sorcerer and perform evil magic. Charms and amulets are widely used to help ward off such magical disease.

All living things have souls which are tiny replicas of the body itself, but in death the human soul leaves the body in the form of a bird. The dead souls live in the west in a spirit world, but they sometimes return with malice toward the living because of some disappointment they experienced on earth. They are greatly feared by the living.

Karei, the god of thunder, is the most prominent member of the spirit world. He is a creator-hero who gave mankind life and the rules of behavior. When thunder is heard it is a sign that Karei is displeased because someone has violated one of his taboos. Someone who has sinned, or who will volunteer to be a scapegoat, must render atonement by gashing his shins and tossing his blood toward the thunder.

Selected Readings. Paul Schebesta, *Among the Forest Dwarfs of Malaya* (London: Hutchinson and Co., n. d.) is a popular account of his stay among the Semang. The author is a well-known specialist on Pygmies and primitive religion. W. W. Skeat and C. O. Blagden, *Pagan Races of the Malay Peninsula* (Two Vols. London: The Macmillan Company, 1906) is an important general source on the peoples of Malaya.

The Andaman Islanders

The Andaman Islands lie along the eastern side of the Bay of Bengal and together with the nearby Nicobar Islands form one of the states of modern India. The climate is tropically warm all year, with heavy rain fall from May through November (the so-called monsoon season) and relatively dry the rest of the time. The dense forests contain wild pigs, the largest animal; reptiles and birds; roots; fruit; nuts; seeds; and honey. Fish, shellfish, the dugong (a large aquatic mammal), and turtles are important dietary items in the coastal areas.

The natives of the islands are Pygmies, much like the Negritos of the Congo and Malaya. They were rather more settled and lived in larger communities than the Semang, however, because of a more abundant food supply. The native population was believed to have been about 5,500 before European diseases began to take their toll. Syphilis, measles, and influenza have ravaged the islands since 1890 and today there are only a few surviving Andamanese.

Technology. Most of the Andamanese knives, scrapers, and arrowpoints were made of shell. For hunting, the Andamanese shunned traps, spears, and poisons and depended entirely on the bow and arrow, which was also used for shooting large fish (small fish were taken in nets). The only equipment used by women in gathering was a sharpened digging stick.

Canoes were hollowed out of a single log, but were often quite large and equipped with outrigger floats to prevent capsizing.

Because the Andamanese were somewhat less nomadic than most hunting-gathering peoples, their housing was better and they used more household implements, even including clay cooking pots. The houses in the main village were single-family, mat-roofed huts left open at the sides, arranged in a rough circle around the communal dance ground. These huts were sturdily built because after being occupied continuously for the several months of the rainy season, they were abandoned for the dry season when the bands were migrating, to be re-occupied later.

Economy and Society. The land over which the band roamed was considered communal property to be defended against outsiders, although like the Semang, individuals held rights over fruit trees. Sharing and hospitality were emphasized, although it seems that the Andamanese were rather more given to the exchange of gifts than most other societies.

The basis of social life in the bands was kinship alone, but the Andamanese seemed to be more loosely organized than most primitive societies. Personal names were used in address, preceded by a term of respect (like our own Sir or Madam) when an elder was addressed; but otherwise the sharp distinctions in relationships were not stressed. An unusual social custom may have been related to this: Children were passed around in adoption very freely so that the ties of social parenthood were more diffused at the same time that they were weakened between the children and the actual parents. The band itself, at least at the time of Radcliffe-Brown's study in 1906–1908, was composite in the sense that exogamy was not insisted on and marital residence rules were informal so that the band was not patrilocal in composition. Levirate and sororate were common kinds of marriage responsibilities, however.

Polity. The Andamanese, like others in our sample, had no formal governmental institutions. Decisions affecting the community were made by the community, although older men may have had somewhat more influence than others. Nor were there any explicit codes of law; antisocial behavior was regulated simply by public opinion. Relations among the various bands were also not formalized. True warfare did not exist, and there was not even much fighting or feuding.

Ideology. The Andamanese were much more isolated than the other forest Pygmies, and as a consequence were ignorant about the world of strangers. Their language is a completely separate stock, with no known affinity to any other. At the time of their discovery by Europeans, it is said that they were completely unaware of the existence of other humans, and believed that the huge strangers were spirits. Another curious gap in their knowledge was that they apparently did not know how to kindle fire, but had to preserve it carefully when migrating. Even their mythological accounts of the origin of fire had a culture-hero create it merely by blowing on some ashes.

The Andamanese shaman had two attributes; he could cure illness and dispel or arouse storms. And of course he could also bring illness on enemies. Like other hunting-gathering societies, the Andamanese peopled the universe with spirits. Some were "big spirits," creator-heroes, and others simply the spirits that animate everything that lives.

Dancing was the most usual art (and entertainment) and also played a prominent part in important ceremonies. Near one end of the central dance ground was placed a convex sounding-board on which the singer would beat out a rhythm with his foot in accompaniment to his song. A row of seated women served as a chorus and also helped beat time by clapping their hands on the hollow formed by their thighs. A row of male dancers coordinated their steps, hopping on one foot for an interval and then the other.

Selected Readings. E. H. Man, "On the Aboriginal Inhabitants of the Andaman Islands," *Journal of the Anthropological Institute,* Vol. XII, London, 1882, is probably the most important source on the Andaman Islanders. Man was for many years an officer of the Penal Settlement at Fort Blair and for four of those years was in charge of the Andamanese Homes, a mission and hospital for the natives.

A. R. Radcliffe-Brown, *The Andaman Islanders* (Glencoe: The Free Press, 1948) is the standard professional ethnographic account of the Andaman Islanders, supplementing Man's work. It is in some way more sophisticated, but Man had the advantages of a longer stay, fuller comprehension of the language, and the fact that at the time of his residence aboriginal culture was more complete and the population not nearly so depleted.

Index

A